MW00834140

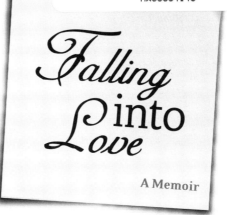

Falling into Love

A Memoir

How an Average
Guy Got the Girl
of His Dreams

Ned Erickson

[RELEVANTBOOKS]

Published by RELEVANT Books
A division of RELEVANT Media Group, Inc.

www. relevantbooks.com
www.relevantmediagroup.com

© 2006 RELEVANT Media Group

Design by RELEVANT Solutions
Cover and Interior design by Ben Pieratt

Library of Congress Control Number: 2005938882
International Standard Book Number: 0-9768175-3-5

For information or bulk orders:
RELEVANT MEDIA GROUP, INC.
100 SOUTH LAKE DESTINY DR., STE. 200
ORLANDO, FL 32810
407-660-1411

06 07 08 09 10 8 7 6 5 4 3 2 1

Printed in the United States of America

To Leela
Love, Ned

Contents

Acknowledgments

In many ways these next lines are my most important because to me, relationships are the most important thing. It has been a joy to write a book where all the characters are those Lia and I love. These pages tell our story—not the entire story, not even most of it, but enough. And I'm sure as you read, you'll get the picture: Lia and I have been blessed with an unfair number of people who care about us. We often quip that we have been cursed with too many friends. This writing project has taught me not only that it is not a curse, but also that there is no such thing as too many.

As I have read these pages over and over, I smile at the sweet friendships we have been given. Your love for us is immeasurable, and we love you all to the moon. However, by the very nature and style of this book, I have also become quite aware of the many who should but do not appear in these pages. If that is the case with you, please know your omission was not intentional and in no way speaks to how much you mean to Lia and me.

With sadness I must write in generalities, but there are a few of you I need to acknowledge by name. First of all, Cara Davis and the family at RELEVANT, thank you for taking a chance on me. Your belief in this book has meant the world, and I am forever grateful.

I must also thank the team of editors who helped me from draft to draft. So many words have changed since that first manuscript, I should call you co-authors. Thank you Tony Abbott, Cynthia Lewis, Brandi Kellett, Matt and Ashley Griffith, Steve Taylor, Geoff and Arika Long, Lindsay Lumpkin, Corene Israel, and Mom and Pops.

Speaking of family, I can't thank you enough, Mom, Pops, Lee, and extended family. Since I can remember, you have made me feel like the most precious person on the planet. I am exceedingly fortunate. I love you with all my heart. And to the Simpson clan, thank you for letting me marry in. I knew I was getting more than I deserved when I married Lia, but I had no idea the fringe benefits I would receive in becoming a Simpson. I love you, Rich, Sue, Gus, Ruth, Cara, Jeremy, Caitlin, Todd, and Chad. You are the greatest.

To my friends in Philly, I have not been back in awhile, but I have often traveled to you in my thoughts and prayers. To my family at Davidson College, thank you for being a part of the crucible time; they were the best and most formative of years. To Young Life, thank you for hiring me straight out of college and teaching me that it is a good thing to be me. To the people of Winston-Salem, you are the hometown I had always hoped for. Thank you for adopting me as your son. To the people of Denver, Lia and I have never been more blessed. Thank you Residents, FCA, Platt Park Posse, Greenwood, Couples Group, and Young Life.

This book was truly inspired by three people. I can't write these next lines without tears filling my eyes. Grandpa and Grandma, Bernie and Le, your love for each other and for our Heavenly Father was one for the ages. I miss you. You are my heroes.

Finally—please forgive me if I get mushy—Lia, my love, I adore you. Thank you for not only allowing me but also encouraging me to write about how we fell into love.

Letter to the Reader

Lia and I met in January of 1998, and we just recently celebrated our fifth anniversary. *Falling* is what happened to us. It is an ordinary story, full of stumbles and false starts and ugly moments. The only truth we have found is what we have tripped over and fallen into. And I guess that's the point.

Love is what happens. It is not something you conjure or create. You cannot manufacture it. You cannot make it happen. It is like falling; it is out of your control. You do not climb into love or fly into love or even walk into it. You *fall* into love; love bruises and bumps and breaks.

Falling is rather painful. You fall down stairs. You fall into the hands of robbers. You fall short. Acorns fall and hit your head. Vases fall and shatter on the floor. Heroes fall. Empires fall. Planes without motors fall. And even if the falling part doesn't get you, the landing part will.

But love is different than stairs and empires and planes without motors. Love bruises and bumps, but it also holds. Love is like a pair of hands. They may break you into a thousand pieces, but they can also put your pieces back together.

At least, that is what happened to Lia and me.

Love has a bit of magic to it. There is more than meets the eye, something supernatural and divine.

You have two people minding their own business, living their own lives, weaving through relationships like one wanders through a bookstore, hoping something will catch their eye and change their life forever. And POOF! Like magic, love happens. Suddenly, she is here, and she opens a door into his heart. He finds his story in hers and she finds her story in his, and they decide their stories are better told if they include each other's. So in a sacred instant, before God and all these witnesses, they say "I do"—and nothing changes (he is still him, and she is still her) yet everything does because mysteriously, two individuals have somehow become one. That is magic.

Reading a book can be magical, too. Has it ever happened to you? You read some simple words on a page, and your heart suddenly swells in resonance with the lines before your eyes. It sings, *Your story is mine, and my story is yours.*

All in an instant, like magic—POOF!—simple words on a page open the door of your heart.

In the pivot of a hinge, in the twinkling of an eye, words open a door into your heart, where you find something you had but didn't know you had or forgot you had or thought you were the only one who had. And as quick as a breath, in simple words on a page, you and I, reader and writer, fall into a state of connection. That is magic, too.

Falling is a true story, true in that these stories actually happened. But what makes them worth reading, I hope, is that they are true for you. And my deepest desire for you, dear reader, is that while you read, magic happens. Your story comes to mind.

May the following simple words on a page open a door into your heart where you find something you have but don't know you have or forgot you have or think you are the only one who has. May this story, in an instant, in the twinkling of an eye, cause us to fall into a glorious state of connection. May that connection bring you hope.

Ned S. Erickson
October 27, 2005

Chapter One
Sure Bet

Lia and I fell in love on a bet. It was a gamble worth the taking, I guess you could say, though at the moment of palm press to palm press, we had little idea that the stakes we were playing for would be so high. Neither of us had a clue this wager would eventually lead to love, to marriage. If we had, I wonder if we would have shaken on it. Only God knows, and as Lia and I have reminisced about how it all came together, we're convinced He must have been the one holding the cards. For on that fateful September day in 1998, I wouldn't have taken 99-to-1 odds that I would end up with Lia Simpson. We were, matrimonially, as long a shot as a hundred-pound girl eating an entire batch of brownies. And as a matter of fact, that is precisely what brought us together—a teeny-weeny girl and a fateful batch of brownies with love baked in the batter.

It wasn't love at first sight for either of us. In regard to our first encounter, I remember nothing. But in my defense, it was dark and I was in love with one of her friends. Lia had just returned from studying abroad in France, and Sarah, the girl I was in love with, had wanted me to meet her.

It was January, the first week of Wake Forest University's second semester, nine months before the bet. Sarah pushed open Lia's dorm room door and introduced me. Lia later said I wore a green fleece and winked at her when I came into the room. I think she was lying, but like I said, I don't remember. She also told me that I went straight for her roommate's guitar and started playing it without asking permission. I forced everyone to listen to a song I had written, claiming I wanted to be a rock star someday. Lia said I sounded full of myself. That, of course, must have been a lie as well. I don't believe I have ever publicly admitted to wanting to be a rock star.

Our paths must have crossed multiple times over the winter and spring; it turned out that Lia was a volunteer for the nonprofit I was working for. But again, I do not recall anything in particular. I suppose I only had eyes for Sarah—that, and Lia did nothing to draw attention to herself.

The week before finals I dumped Sarah. It was rather unexpected, even for me. When she asked me why, I shrugged my shoulders, and that was it. She started crying; I gripped her elbow and said, "Good luck on your tests." I'm pretty sure by the look on her face that my answer didn't satisfy.

Unfortunately, if Sarah asked me the same question today— why—I would still be unable to answer satisfactorily. Something just wasn't there. Whether that something had to do with her or me, I don't know. I only knew I was done dating Sarah. Our relationship was like a present (aren't they all?). Just as I do with presents, I threw our relationship in the corner pile when I was done playing with it. But I couldn't tell her that. It would make me sound like a jerk.

Sarah's friends didn't appreciate what I had done. They huddled to her side and, with growing animosity, began telling stories about an evil, freckle-faced redhead named Ned who stomped on the hearts of innocent women. Hence, as May moved into June and faded into summer, I watched with horror as these females defamed my name and created the dark society known as the Ned-Haters League (the NHL)—their president, none other than Lia Simpson.

Over the ensuing months, she rallied quite a following. Turns out that women everywhere had similar opinions. As tenderhearted and sweet as Lia appeared, she certainly could make me sound bad.

Consequently, I slowly sailed in the dating doldrums with not a fish in the sea. I went into a period of social hibernation, meeting only with peevish looks and regrettable remarks at my companion-ship attempts. It was a lonely time, and as I look back, I deserved it—all the whispers and giggles, the angled eyebrows, the sideways shaking of heads. I deserved all the pain those glances inflicted; I had toyed with love without realizing the danger. I was the kid sticking the fork in the outlet. I was the boy touching the flames for the first time. I was the student taking the exam without ever reading the book. I hadn't learned the lessons of love. I hadn't fallen into it yet.

Instead, I felt sorry for myself. I was a martyr, another innocent soldier standing before the shooting squad of feminism. Why was everyone so mad at me, anyway? If they really believed I was as bad as they were saying, they should be happy I broke up with Sarah.

Only now do I realize these folks were out for my good. They were trying to help me see; the problem was that I hadn't yet dis-covered I was blind.

Finally, a friend sat me down and told it to me straight. "Ned," he said, "don't take this the wrong way, but you treat girls like crap. The fact is, you are the turd, and you need to be flushed."

"Thanks," I said, as I punched him in the gut.

"Don't mention it," he grunted.

At least I didn't punch him in the face. And I did appreciate his candor.

The lonely summer went by. Lia was beginning her senior year at Wake Forest; I was into my second year mentoring high-school students with the nonprofit. It was early September, time for our overnight leader training. Some beyond-generous board members had offered us their weekend getaway—a house on Lake Norman, about forty-five minutes from Winston-Salem, North Carolina. It had long decks, a dock, and all the accessories you could imagine—and it could accommodate all fifty of us, as long as we lined our sleeping bags next to each other like sardines. It was heaven on earth.

I drove down with Mark, one of the few friends I had left, and as we circled the cloverleaf at the Troutman exit on I-77, he updated me on what our college leaders had been doing over the summer. He spouted off stats like he was a *SportsCenter* host, and I was trying to keep it all straight when, abruptly, in mid-sentence, he paused.

"Uh …" he said, "Lia's going to be here."

"That's all right, Mark. She won't ruin our fun."

"You don't seem to understand. She really doesn't like you, Ned."

"I know. No girls like me," I admitted. I felt my heart twist.

"Ned, she *really* doesn't like you. Like, more than the others. When I told her I was driving down with you, she got this look on her face. I can't even describe it."

"Well, thanks for telling me, I guess. All I have to say is, who cares? If Lia has a problem with me, then that's her deal. I'm not going to have some dumb girl get in the way of my good time."

Mark shook his head.

The weekend was beautiful. The water was shining diamonds, its temperature warm as a bathtub, the colors deep and thick. The sky was Carolina blue, and the trees were green and shaking like a baby rattle. We spent the whole day either in the water or laying out by it. Later that night, the boys carried towels and birthday suits to the dock for a swim; while we skinny-dipped, the girls crept to the water's edge and stole all our coverings. In retaliation, once the girls were asleep, we confiscated their bras and underwear and froze them into a block. I don't remember much training going on. I don't remember much else at all, except laughing in my sleeping bag at the sound of squealing girls chiseling ice cubes out of their panties.

That's about it—oh, and the business about the brownies.

As the weekend waned and most of the cleaning was done, only a few people remained. Mark and I were "supervising" the final tidying touches in the kitchen while Mary, Suzie, and Lia did the work.

"You missed a spot," I encouraged from my ceramic countertop director's chair.

"Make sure you use a moist paper towel to collect the crumbs around the toaster," Mark instructed.

Lia and her friends ignored us and finished up.

They were scooping up one last mound of dirt when, to our surprise, the oven *ding*ed.

"What's that?" I asked.

"The oven (you moron)," Lia said in a condescending tone. She had been sponging the island, but now moved toward the stove.

Cracking the door open, the sweet waft of brownies hit Lia full in the face and in seconds filled the house.

"Mmm, brownies," she said with an upward arc to her lip. "I'm so hungry I could eat the whole batch."

"Whatever," I scoffed to Mark.

Sensing a challenge, she turned toward me and glared. "Yeah, I could. You don't know how hungry I am."

"Look at you," I returned. She was teeny—barely five foot four, maybe 110 pounds when wet, wearing lead boots, and carrying two sacks of flour. It was a physical impossibility. I dismissed her hyperbole with a sideways sway of my chin.

"You don't know," she sneered.

I leaned back. "Well, there is only one way to find out. Eat them.

I bet you can't even eat twelve."

There was a general hum at the anticipation of a standoff. Mary and Suzie put down the broom and dustpans and moved to Lia's side. One of their own needed them.

Lia gained confidence upon their arrival. "Yes, I can. What do I get when I win?"

I started thinking. *Hmmm, what would really get her goat? What would feel like a dagger in her NHL little heart? Laundry for a month? No, too revealing. Money? Nah, neither of us has any …*

Then it came to me: "All right. The loser has to buy an airbrushed T-shirt with a big heart and the other person's name on the front."

The audience laughed and howled approval.

Caught up in the ululation, I added, "Oh, and on the back, the number four and then the word 'ever.' Real redneck-like. And you have to wear it every day for a week, no matter what."

Her face turned scarlet. Whether she was blushing or boiling, to this day I don't know.

The girls moved in close behind her like a boxing entourage. I slid to my feet with Mark, my one-man posse, at my back. Lia and I squared off at the center of the ring, the quadrangle of dessert.

Mary, a devout Lia-lover, began sending verbal jabs: "Don't listen to Ned—or should we call him *Nerd*?"

"Hey, you stay out of this!" Mark snapped in my defense.

The brownies smelled delicious. A wisp of steam rose like a genie referee and held us at arm's length.

Lia was all business. "Twelve brownies, you said?"

"Yep, but I get to cut them."

"No, I want an impartial cutter." She looked around. "Like Mary."

"Mary's not impartial; she hates me! Tell you what—I'll cut them, but everyone has to agree on the size. And since I'm a nice guy, I will give you thirty minutes, and you can drink whatever you want. Just one rule: you are not allowed to puke. Any heavage will constitute immediate disqualification."

Mark grunted support. The girls were silent.

Without hesitation, she shoved her teeny-weeny hand in my direction; I placed mine around hers. We shook. It was official.

Both teams stirred in the buzz.

"It's a bet." Lia straddled a stool and narrowed her eyes. "Grab a knife, Suzie. Mark, get me a glass of milk."

Mark opened the fridge, chose whole milk over the half-gallon of skim beside it, and filled a tall glass.

Suzie handed the knife to me, and I started cutting. Four pairs of eyes looked on, Lia's the largest and growing by the cut. All unanimously agreed at the first incision, a fair, wallet-sized square section. However, the girls gulped in unison as they extrapolated that twelve brownies made up at least three-quarters of the pan.

Lia was quiet. Could she really do it? I noticed droplets of sweat gathering near her temples.

After completing the grid, to demonstrate my compassion and remove possible technicality, I pressed the knife around the perimeter to aid access to each piece. Finishing the final cut, I stepped away.

"Okay, Lia. It is six thirty. You have until seven o'clock to finish those brownies."

The atmosphere was intense. The bet was on. I was sure I'd win.

Lia, with a lift of her finger, dislodged the first piece.

Four were gone in five minutes.

Eight were gone in thirteen. She had finished one glass of milk and clinked the countertop for another. She looked unstoppable. The last three she had eaten in stride. I wished I had dared her to eat the whole thing. She really could do it.

But one bite into the ninth piece, her momentum began to waver. Her once-voracious chews now seemed under tranquilizer sedation. Her vermilion complexion grew pale, then into shades of avocado. Swallowing, she put the rest of nine down. Her tongue clicked thick off the roof of her mouth. Tiny forearm muscles flinched as her hands gripped the island. She had hit the proverbial wall. She had bonked. She was entering the twilight zone of sugar overdose.

Opportunity knocked. "Hey, Mark," I said loudly, "man, I could really go for some lukewarm mayonnaise and cottage cheese right about now."

Mark caught on and contributed to the volley. "Oh yeah, how about some raw sausage links?"

"Stop it," scowled Suzie.

We didn't.

"And some wet, soggy bacon on moldy bread."

"Cut it out."

"I'm thirsty. Can I have a glass of armpit sweat?" added Mark, taking the gross-ocity to a new level.

"You're starting to make me gag," I giggled.

Lia wobbled to her feet. It was 6:51 p.m., and five full minutes had ticked by without a mouthful.

"Are you throwing in the towel?" I asked.

"Just resting," said Lia, slurring slightly like Rocky Balboa between water squirts.

I could almost taste the aerosol, smell the mist, read the spray-painting on the wall.

"You know, you don't look so good," I said, feigning concern.

"You never look good," she blasted back.

Everyone cheered at the comeback, even Mark. Something in the tenor of his laughter hinted at treason. Lia sensed it, too.

She also sensed the pendulum of momentum swinging back in her direction, moving with the tide of general opinion.

Mark shuffled discreetly away from my corner, but I noticed. I was alone. If I were the kind of guy who listened to his heart, I would have realized it was jumping ship as well. It liked the girl with the bloated belly; it wanted her to win.

The applause calmed Lia's insides. She arched her back and

explored her stomach for space with her fingers. She jogged a lap around the island, sending her supporters, new and old, into a frenzy. She sat back down, took a deep swig of milk, and put the rest of brownie number nine into her mouth for emphasis and effect.

"Li-a! Li-a! Li-a!" chanted the chorus.

In no time, she was through half of brownie ten. Two more to go, and there was no stopping her—eleven down; twelve going, going—she swallowed, opened her mouth, and stuck out her tongue—two brown streaks spanning from her incisors to her molars were the only evidence of her accomplishment. She had downed them all. She had won the bet ...

... And walked straight to the bathroom.

"She's puking!" I stammered. "She lost!"

I followed her into the toilet to witness.

"Get out! I just have to pee," she said, stiff-arming me with her teeny right hand.

"All right, but I'm standing next to the door. Don't try to pull any funny stuff. I can hear everything going on in there."

All I heard was a stream.

"Don't turn on the faucet to hide anything!" I warned.

"Shut up." *Flush*. She turned the knob and walked on by.

Whether to further my humiliation or for some other hidden reason, Lia decided to go with me to purchase my punishment. Locating an airbrush artist, however, proved more difficult than either Lia or I had expected. We searched the mall. We sought advice from the people at the Piercing Pagoda and the craftsman at the Customized License Plate Boutique. We perused the phonebook, but to no avail—there was nothing under *T-shirt*, *paint*, or *rural apparel*. It seemed the airbrush-design artisan was a dying breed. It seemed perhaps we would not find what we were looking for.

But at the same time, we found something else. Through the experience, Lia and I became friends. We spent an hour reading sappy Hallmark cards in strange accents to each other. I learned of her insatiable appetite for gumballs, and she learned that I made Orange Juliuses in seventh-grade cooking class. I began to hope that we'd never find an airbrush T-shirt shop, that we'd go on forever like this. I felt something not unlike attraction. She started to feel I wasn't so bad after all. I was intrigued by her never-say-die attitude, her sense of humor, her ability to eat huge amounts of food. She appreciated my muscular frame, my magnetic personality, my machismo.

Nah, she just liked beating me.

We finally caught wind of a Spray and Pay at the local Saturday morning flea market. Twelve dollars and a cultural experience later, I was parading around in a classic Fruit of the Loom, a heart professing my devotion to a former archenemy named Lia, and neon-green words spelling out "4-ever" across my shoulder blades. I wore that T-shirt all week—to meetings, to exercise, to soccer practice, to bed.

Publicly, I despised it. Privately, it was one of the coolest threads I had ever donned.

The foreshadowing could not have been more potent, and, looking back, it's impossible not to recognize the richness of the irony. I lost the bet but won the gal. Some bets you can't lose.

I wonder what would have happened had Lia not swallowed those last fragments of brownie batter? Only God knows, and like I said, He was dealing the cards. For Love must have been baked in those brownies that day. A pinch of Providence mixed in with the chocolate chunks. A dash of Destiny added to the cups of sugar. A tablespoon of Fortune included with the vanilla. And a whole lot of Fate in the flour. That you can bet on.

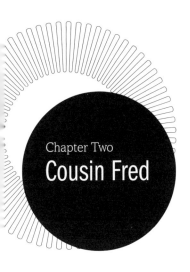

Summers were hot, winters were cold, but it was fall—so as Goldilocks would say, it was just right. But we're not talking porridge; we're talking my old apartment—that attic space above the Turners' garage with barely enough room to fit a bed, couch, microwave, dorm refrigerator, bookshelf, and me. And as long as you didn't mind the dust seeping through the floorboards, the voyeuristic squirrels watching you sleep through the yellow-stained skylight, the erratic electric heater clicking and clacking in a vain attempt to mimic the feats of the Little Engine, and the occasional roach, it was heaven on earth.

Actually, I think there was only one roach. But he was everywhere, and he was huge. Gargantuan. I'm not exaggerating—his abdomen alone spanned the length of my middle finger. He had wings the size of a bird—and not a hummingbird, mind you, a big one. His head—well, it looked like an eight ball. My cockroach had *Guinness Book* written all over him. He was a sight to behold, and you could not help but see him.

Once, I tried to exterminate him by smacking him with a *Sports Illustrated*. But when I lifted the magazine to check for carnage, there he was, sitting with hardly a scratch.

I gaped as I watched his glassy eyes turn to look at me, as if to say, *If you know what's good for you, you will NEVER do that again!*

Cockroach walked away, his polished head shaking in a "people these days!" motion.

I stood, stunned, watching my insect roommate waddle his fat self under the left leg of my plaid couch. My magazine weapon uncurled in my hand, and I stared in jaw-drop disbelief at this creature's resilience. Those things are indestructible. No wonder they can survive a nuclear holocaust.

I never engaged in combat with Cockroach again. Every once in a while I would shift a cushion and interrupt his napping or open a book and catch him reading or looking at pictures. But we mostly kept to ourselves and stayed out of each other's way. On the whole, Roach and I cohabited quite nicely.

In fact, one night while I was playing guitar on the corner of my bed, singing to the dust mites on my lampshade, he and I even became friends.

For no particular reason, I was singing with notable passion that evening. As I strummed, I closed my eyes and pictured an arena full of swaying fans and swooning women. On the last chord, the corners of my lips curled to the skylight, and I raised my hand in salute like a true rock star. I could almost hear the crowd's roar, and I basked in the moment. But when I opened my eyes back to my lonely reality, I realized I was not alone. There he was, a foot away from my knee, spectating from a green plaid square on the cushion nearest me. Sitting and watching, watching and listening. *Cockroach had been listening! I didn't even know they had ears!* The thought melted my heart.

"I didn't know I had a real audience tonight," I said to Roach. "You want to hear another?"

He settled back on his hind legs as if to say, *Bring it on.*

So I started a song I had written about Oreo cookies and sang it to my roommate and new friend. Cockroach bobbed his head back and forth to the beat. I named him Fred.

But I digress. Where was I? Oh yes, it was fall, beautiful and warm. Goldilocks-warm—the kind of temperature that holds you like your mother did, when peace comes in a quiet breeze, and air begs to be taken in lungfuls. It was a lovely day, a day that nourished. And I was lying on my bed, my skylight serving as a magnifying glass in the afternoon sun—and I the metaphorical ant getting fried. The moving leaves above were sifting sunrays; it looked like a thousand diamonds in a dazzling dance. Mmmm, it was beautiful warm.

And I was in the best of moods because I was waiting for Lia.

It was two weeks after the brownie bet, and we were still on our T-shirt treasure hunt. At one point during our last excursion, conversation had shifted gears to bike riding, so it was only gentlemanly to ask her if she wanted to come over after class and go for an Indian summer land cruise on a pair of two-wheeled chariots. Once Lia had figured out what I was talking about, she had accepted without coercion, which put a smile on my face and no small delight in my heart.

Feet ascended the side staircase; in a moment I heard knocking, and in another Lia was making herself at home on my plaid couch (her tush settling into the very same spot previously occupied by my friend Fred—but I didn't tell her and never will).

It was her first time to my penthouse shanty, so I sat up in bed and gave her "the tour"—a point to the right: "that's the bathroom"; a point to the back wall: "that's the kitchen"; a point to the bookshelf: "the entertainment center"; a point to her and Fred's cushion: "the living room"; and a point to the place I was sitting: "the bedroom."

Lia played with the hair behind her ear and smiled. She was wearing a brown shirt, khaki shorts, and two tanned and toned legs. She brought her face to the autumn sun. And when she looked at me, her eyes caught a sunbeam and did a dazzle-dance of their own. She was beautiful. That was the moment I first noticed.

But I tried my best to conceal it. "So, how do you like the place?" I asked.

Giving the room a once-over, she paused, considered, then said the unexpected: "This room kind of reminds me of Cousin Fred."

Cousin Fred! Did she just say "Cousin Fred"? I gulped. *How does she know about Fred?* My shirt collar started feeling uncomfortable. In a panic, I surveyed the room, searching the shadows, peering into the crevices, looking for a sign of my roommate.

Fred was nowhere to be found, but the idea that he was around and that Lia might have spied him sent me shifting nervously from butt cheek to butt cheek.

Frantically, my eyes continued to dart about the room. My hands grabbed two fistfuls of blanket, and my mind angrily thought, *If Fred shows even an antenna, I'm going to kill him for real this time.*

Lia detected the uneasiness in my countenance and lifted an eyebrow.

I looked back at her uncomfortably. Her hands were calmly laced around her knee.

Her serenity perplexed me. I knew she was a biology major, but if she had seen Cousin Fred—is that what she called him, cousin?—she would be acting differently. No ordinary girl could be this relaxed at the sight of a cigar-sized cockroach.

Either she was the Jane Goodall of the insect world, or she hadn't seen him, I conjectured. I determined to keep an eye out. But in the meantime, I took a deep breath and decided to play it cool.

"Ahem. Cousin Fred, you said? Who's ... er ... Cousin Fred?"

"I can't tell you," Lia answered curtly.

"What do you mean, you can't tell me?" God, was she pretty.

"It's a secret."

"Well, if it's a secret, why did you mention it?" I asked.

She leaned back into the couch and crossed her smooth legs.

"You're right. I shouldn't have said anything. Please forgive me."

"No can do. You let the cat out of the bag; you can't get it back in that easy."

"Yes, I can. I promised I wouldn't tell anybody." All of a sudden she was the one getting nervous, and I liked it.

Cockroach or not, my curiosity was itching and needed a scratch. The mystery behind this Fred fellow was too much for me. I bounced to the end of the bed and put my elbows to my knees.

"Whom did you promise?" I prodded.

"The other people who know about him," she answered.

"You mean there are others? What's so special about them? I bet everyone knows. You just won't tell me because you like ticking me off." I hated being left in the dark.

"That's not true," she said.

"You think you are so much better than me, don't you? You are dangling Cousin Fred over my head like a carrot, and I'm the donkey that's never going to get a nibble. You're just stringing me along." I huffed, pretending to be perturbed.

Lia brought her other leg to her lap and crossed her arms in a matching fold of their own. Closed off in double Indian-style, she answered, "Listen, only my sisters know about Cousin Fred. And we pinky-swore that we would never tell anyone about him."

"Oh." I could appreciate a sisters' pact. Still, I wanted in. Bending forward, I switched my voice knob to Richard Gere Smooth and gave her a look through the bangs of my hair. "Come on," I needled.

"Well, we did say we could each tell two people."

"Oh! How many people have you told?"

"One."

"Well, all right. I'm ready; lay it on. Who is this mystery man?"

"You see …" Lia tried to let me down easy. "We agreed that we would only tell two people: our best friend, and the man we were going to marry."

"So you told Cameron?" I asked. Cameron was her best friend and roommate through college.

"Yes."

"So, how do you know I'm not 'the one'?"

Lia's face twisted. "What did you say?"

What did I say? *How do you know I'm not "the one"?* The One! I felt my face flush in embarrassment. *Oh my gosh! I just asked Lia, the woman who just two weeks earlier hated my guts, if she thought I was "the one"!*

Lia frowned.

I wanted to apologize. Tell her that it just came out. That I didn't mean it. It was one of those comments created in the subconscious. Honestly, the thought had never crossed my mind. It had slipped out before I realized what I was saying. But I kept silent. For some reason, I didn't want to take it back.

Later, months down the road, Lia related to me that when I uttered "the one," the room had started spinning, all went vertigo, and she almost threw up.

I asked her, "So what do you think that means?"

She smiled and said, "There's no telling."

All I remember is that she was quiet for quite some time; she hid her near-upheaval well in the poor lighting of my room.

We sat, awkward, for an eternity—somewhere around thirty seconds.

I didn't know what to say. Lia glanced at her watch, and I realized that if I didn't do something quickly, she would probably make up some reason to leave. I hopped to my feet and stretched.

"Hey, how about we ride those two-wheeled chariots?"

"Sure," she sighed, happy to finally have a change of subject. Besides, the fresh air would do her good.

Outside, we mounted our bikes and rode off in the beautiful, warm autumn afternoon. We crossed Buena Vista Avenue, straight down Archer, and across Coliseum Boulevard. We entered the grounds of Graylyn Conference Center, where we leaned our backs and bikes on the arch of a stone bridge and became better friends.

We were shocked at how long we talked; still, Lia almost apologized when she said she had to go. We high-fived goodbye. Her honey-brown legs straddled her turquoise beach cruiser, and I smiled while I watched her calves flex at each pedal press.

Just before she rode out of sight, she glanced back and fluttered her fingers in the air. I waved my arm like a reed in the sway and remained on the bridge for a long moment. I closed my eyes and, on the back of my lids, envisioned more days like this. The image looked good.

I tucked that mental photograph like a bookmark in my mind. A year and a half later, on a beautiful, warm February afternoon, I proposed to Lia in the shadow of the arch beside that stone bridge. A month after that, I met Cousin Fred. Guess I was "the one" after all. I'd tell you who Fred is, but I'm sworn to secrecy. What I can tell you is that *he* is not human either.

I never told Lia about my own Fred. It seems we can both keep secrets … at least for a while.

Fred, wherever you are, I hope you are doing well. And if you ever read this someday, thanks for keeping me company, and thanks for keeping quiet when Lia called your name that day.

Hope you're enjoying all those things cockroaches do, whatever they are. And someday, after we humans blow ourselves to smithereens in a final nuclear holocaust, when it is just you and all the other roaches, remember me with a smile. Remember that guy who once tried and failed to kill you. Remember that guy who used to sing you songs. And on those warm evenings, as you huddle your family in the alcoves of radioactive cardboard, as you watch the sun fade into the fallout wasteland, as you feel a gentle urge to look through the mental photographs of your own memory, hum a little diddy for me.

Chapter Three
Treasure

I am a dromedary, a camel caravanning through the desert of life. I carry baggage like a hump on my back, the weight of past relationships, broken hearts, and misplaced desires. And I can't seem to get rid of it. Everything I've done is still there in my heart and memory and on the back of my eyelids.

By the time I met Lia, my dromedary hump was about the size of a Volkswagen Beetle. By my twenty-fifth birthday two years later, I had failed at love so many times that I had honestly lost count. Put in baseball terms, if success in dating were a batting average, I would have been sent to the minors a long time ago.

Before marriage (BM), I treated my heart like crap. I let it wander aimlessly about, allowing it to do whatever it wanted and latch on to whomever it willed. My heart was as thirsty for love as a nomad is for an oasis. After marriage (AM) the situation is not much different, but in my BM days, I thought differently. I thought that if and when—whether by happenstance or some device of my own making—I tricked a girl into loving me, all my burdens would disappear, all my past would melt away like ice. I was sure that once I met "the one," all my troubles and heartaches would be behind me. All I had to do was find her—find her and trick her.

And so, from the third grade, when I secretly pledged my eternal love to Stephanie Fitzpatrick during a kickball game, to the present, I was on a continual lookout. I was a sniper. The woman sitting next to a vacant seat on an airplane, the ringless lady testing apples in the produce department of the supermarket, the passion-and-purity girl praising the almighty and merciful Father on Sunday morning—they were all considered through my cross hairs. This is embarrassing to admit, but I could be in a convenience store lifting a Yoo-hoo! from behind a fogging glass door and, out of the corner of my eye, perceive a woman's presence from behind another fogging glass door down the row. In ten seconds I could (in my mind) pick her up, go on a series of dates, propose, get married, have 2.5 kids, become grandparents, join a retirement community, and die.

Most of the time, this imaginary relationship remained in my imagination; the few relationships that actually materialized never followed the aforementioned formula. I always ended up hurt, whether or not I was the one who broke it off. (I am honestly unsure which side of the breakup hurts more. Regardless of how a relationship ends, it will always be painful and leave us with more broken pieces to add to the baggage already on our backs. I guess that's why they call it a breakup.)

Therefore, by the time I was a quarter-century old, my heart held a lot of weight. I had gone out with so many girls that I, embarrassingly, could not remember all their names. I had fallen in love with one in particular who, after a two-year relationship, proceeded to cheat on me with a random guy. And I had dated another girl (whom I've already mentioned), who informed me that she was worse off after having known me. Those were merely a few of my burdens. I was broken and sensitive and wounded and calloused and struggling and confused and lost, as perhaps you have been at some point. At least, most of you.

Most ... because there are probably some of you who are like Lia.

She was so pure. She had never been in love. She had never dated. She had never been kissed, except by her parents. I still have a hard time believing this. Somehow, my beautiful bride survived, unscathed, the hive of hormones that is high school and college.

I just didn't get it. How could someone so sweet, so cute, so fun, so great ... so wonderful ... so awesome (words fail me)—how did someone like Lia fly under the radar for so long? The world may never know, as the old Tootsie Roll ads used to say. How—with her big brown eyes (she thinks they're green); her gentle, slender fingers (she thinks they're wrinkly); her intriguing smile (with her fake left front tooth that glows a funny color under black light; she lost her real tooth while horseback riding)—did she never seem to turn a head? How—with her sense of humor, MCAT-acing mind, deep kindness, and much more—was Lia never approached by anyone? And yet, her beauty had eluded me as well. She was a diamond in the rough, whatever that means, a geode that hadn't broken open. She was a buried treasure.

Jesus talked about the kingdom of heaven being like a treasure hidden in a field, so valuable that it was worth selling everything you had in order to purchase it. Lia, to me, was a treasure like that, hidden in a field. Once I unearthed it, once I saw Lia for the treasure that she is, it didn't take long to realize that being with her would be worth more than everything I had.

The way I saw it, by some set of strange, unexplainable circumstances or by some wicked wizard's spell, Lia's true value had been buried, and I, by dumb luck, happened to be the first to stumble upon it. So, like the man in the parable, my discovery compelled me to go to town, cash in all my dating chips, and purchase the field in which she was hidden—even if it cost me everything I had. And in a way, it did. Marriage, after all, is an all-or-nothing proposition—or should be.

Sometimes I treat Lia like an acquisition; I fool myself into believing I actually deserve a treasure as precious as her. Those are the foolish times, the times I forget she is a gift, a priceless one.

———————————

We were driving to Virginia Beach. It was the last day of 1999, hours away from the new millennium and the potential attack of the dreaded Y2K bug. Lia and I, six months into our relationship, were heading to the ocean to celebrate with friends the death of all computerized devices. My heart felt like a swollen cloud. My heaviness, however, wasn't due to sorrow over the end of modern civilization, but rather to the two-ton weight of a dromedary hump I was carrying around.

Our relationship had been fantastic up until New Year's Eve. Though we had never talked about it, we both sensed we were steadily heading toward proposal, engagement, marriage, 2.5 kids, grandparenthood, retirement community, and death. But lately, something else had been growing, too. My hump. I could see Lia trying to look at it when we were together. She knew there were things in my past that I was hiding. How could she not? And I wasn't hiding them very well; every time I was with her, my hump tagged along. It was the elephant in the room—or the camel, to keep with the metaphor.

And for the last hour, along U.S. 58 East, we had been rather quiet because I knew she wanted to talk about it.

I hate silence. I also hate confession ... apparently, I hate silence more.

"Lia, we've got to talk," I finally blurted out. Thunder rumbled inside my chest cavity.

"I love you," she replied.

"You what?"

"Love you. I just want you to know that I love you, no matter what."

I felt like I was on the edge of a cliff. "Oh. Well, you might think differently if you knew how messed up I am."

Lia didn't say anything. She just listened.

"I've done a lot of things I'm not very proud of. I mean, I've done a lot of things with girls. A lot of things I wish I hadn't done ... and I know you have such a clean past."

Lia's eyes started to water.

"I feel ashamed. I wish I didn't have so much baggage, Lia. You deserve better."

"No, I don't," she whispered.

"Yes, you do. You don't know all I've done. You don't want to know."

Lia sniffed and said, "Yes, I do."

"You want to know? Lia—"

"Tell me everything," she commanded, her voice gaining strength.

I took a deep breath and exhaled. "Are you sure?"

"Ned." Her tone was tender and serious.

It was a hazy day. Driving to the beach in the winter seemed wrong—about as wrong as I had treated hearts over the years.

"Ned, I love you."

"I love you, too."

The tires clicked every second or two on the cement seams of U.S. 58.

It was like she read my mind. "Whatever it is you need to say, I want you to know you're forgiven." She paused and considered. "And no matter what, I want to be with you."

I believed her, and her confidence gave me courage. I said, "There are a lot of things I've done with girls that I'm ashamed of. I just have all this baggage, and it weighs me down. Maybe if I let it out, it will go away."

"Ned, I know it isn't easy—for either of us. And I can't promise I won't be upset. But I can promise that I will love you."

And just like that, like the doctor she would one day become, Lia performed open-hump surgery. There in the car, heading east on U.S. 58, I opened my mouth, and my hump burst like a nasty, oozy boil. I confessed everything. I sounded like Chunk in the movie *The Goonies* when he told the Fratelli family every bad thing he had ever done, upchuck noises and all. I told her everything—everything I had ever done with every girl I had ever been with. Every wreck of a relationship, every painful breakup—I laid it all out on the dashboard. It was exhausting. I was tired afterward, and sweat was sliding from my forehead.

And when I was done, aside from the humming of wheels on the grooves of the road, there was silence.

Lia angled her body toward the passenger-side rearview mirror. I thought to myself, *She said she'd forgive me, but she didn't know what she was saying. You sure messed this up, Ned. Lia's the best thing that's ever happened to you, and here you go again, ruining it. Another relationship down the toilet.*

"I'm sorry," I said.

"I'm not upset," she said through tears.

The irony made me smile. "Could have fooled me."

"I'm not upset at you."

Huh? Confused, I asked, "Then what are you upset about?"

Lia took a deep breath and exhaled. "I'm not as wonderful as you think I am. I've got crap in my closet, too."

"No, you don't."

"Yes, as a matter of fact, I do."

She began to talk, and to my astonishment, it turned out that she was a dromedary as well. For twenty-two years, she too had been accumulating her own burdens like a hump on her back. I gripped the steering wheel, stunned, as she began unpacking her baggage before my eyes—the baggage of countless, nameless rejections; of not being asked to the dance; of listening to her friends talk about the boys they were dating; of being alone on Friday night; of never being held, never being touched, never being wanted. She had felt invisible, overlooked, worthless. She had the baggage of self-hatred, self-injury, and self-destruction. And by the time she was halfway through, I realized Lia's heart was as broken as mine or anyone else's.

We were close to the beach house when she finished, minutes away from our friends, but miles away from any desire to celebrate. I pulled to the side of the road, several blocks short of our destination. We embraced, and Lia continued to cry. I held her tightly, wishing my own eyes would well up and spill over. My tear ducts often malfunction.

"Maybe we were meant for each other," I said. I felt her body soften. I stroked her hair until the sound of her tears ceased and was replaced by the gentle, rhythmic percussion of waves at evening tide.

"Do you forgive me?" she asked.

For what? I thought. "Sure thing," I said.

The things we have done, the things we haven't—they are equally damaging, I discovered.

I wish I could erase every memory. I wish I could take back every kiss, every word. I wish I could take back every thing I've ever done with a girl. I wish I could take back every dream, every fantasy, every self-pleasure. I wish I could take it all back. I wish I could have given it all to Lia, as Lia has done to me. I wish I could have met Lia earlier and somehow saved her from all her hurt. I wish life wasn't so painful. I wish boys and girls were not so evil toward one another. We play with hearts like we play with GI Joes and Barbie dolls. In our ignorance, we do not know the difference.

We are all dromedaries, camels caravanning through the desert of life. Some carry the burdens of things done; some carry weights of other kinds.

That is the desert of our lives, the expanse visible to others. That is often how we see ourselves—worthless, meaningless, sick, ugly, unwanted, unloved.

But what I've come to believe is that I was right about Lia all along. Sure, she has lived a desert life, an existence that the world and the devil have done their best to devastate. And on some level they have succeeded: they have landed their blows, inflicted their wounds, and added to the weight. They have hung No Trespassing signs, tried to conceal the evidence, dug holes and covered them up—but they couldn't change the truth. Lia is a treasure.

And as Lia says, if she is treasure, that's proof positive that we all are. There, inside our fields, hidden within each one of us, is a treasure. You are a treasure! I am a treasure! There is a treasure in us all! And the treasure is priceless. If a dozen or a dozen dozens walk by without recognizing it, they are the fools. And their ignorance doesn't change the treasure's value. A thousand could pass and not notice, and the desert life may rise and cover your heart like a dune, like a dromedary hump. But don't lose hope, for Someone sees you.

This Someone knows about your treasure, for He was the One who put it there—and the One who paid everything to get it back. He has the very deed carved into His hands. At this exact moment, He is preparing a place for you, His treasure, and one day He will come to take His treasure home.

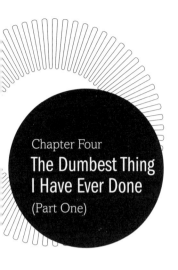

"You have to tell that one," Lia said one evening over dinner.

"I don't have to do anything." We had been talking about *Falling Into Love*.

"I know. But if you are going to write about us, you have to write that."

"That story is not about us; it's about me. It's tangential. It's like a mutant third arm or something."

"But it's unbelievable."

"Exactly. Who's going to believe it? Folks are going to think I made it up."

"No, they aren't."

"I would."

"So?"

"You just want me to write it because you like embarrassing me. I thought wives were supposed to support their husbands. Build them up. Make them look good."

Lia thought for a moment. "If you don't tell that story, then I forbid you to write about me," she said smiling, knowing she had the leverage.

"What? You listen to me, Lia. I'm writing the story, so I can write what I want."

"If you write about me, I'll sue."

"Sue your husband? That's ridiculous."

"Don't call me ridiculous."

"Lia, let's be reasonable. I'm writing our story. I can't write a story about marriage and not include a wife."

"And you can't write our story without telling that one."

She was right.

"You're a punk," I humphed.

"You're a chicken."

"No I'm not."

"Bawk, bawk!" she squawked, as she scraped the rest of her food onto my plate and carried the dishes to the kitchen.

I clucked in my chair.

Honestly, this story isn't necessary.

I suppose none of them are. Necessary, that is. Our stories, our lives aren't necessary. The Great Story, the one that began ten thousand or ten billion or however many years ago, will be told with or without our participation.

And yet my story happened ... and so did yours. You are here; you are alive. And that's significant. For some reason, you have been included as a character in the Great Story. And you may not be necessary, but you certainly are significant.

All the same, surely not every story needs to be written. At the end of the Gospel of John, the disciple confesses, "Jesus did many other things as well. If every one of them were written down, I suppose that even the whole world would not have room for the books that would be written" (21:25, TNIV). We're talking Jesus, who is far cooler than me, whose stories are far more interesting than mine, and whose life was far more necessary than any of ours. And yet, John didn't feel the pressure to record them all.

Even in the court of law, a witness might swear to tell the truth, the whole truth, and nothing but the truth—but still, she only has to answer the questions she is asked. She doesn't have to tell everything.

Lia, you are cruel and unusual.

I mean, do people really want to know about my lowest low, the most humiliating experience of my life, the dumbest thing I have ever done? That Lia insist I write it shows her sense of humor (or lack thereof). Reader, do me a favor and skip the next two chapters. I promise you won't miss a thing.

Why are you still reading? Ugh. Fine. Don't say I didn't warn you. You will never think the same of me again. Lia, you are a punk ... and I guess I am a chicken.

It was over the Christmas of 1999, about ten days before open-hump surgery, when I grew feathers.

As I wrote in the last chapter, Lia and I had been dating since August, and our relationship was fantastic; it had been rolling along like a pair of two-wheeled chariots on a beautiful, warm afternoon. Sure, there were things that still needed to be addressed, but for the most part, all systems were a go. Therefore, in accordance with cultural protocol and current standards of etiquette, our impending sixth-month mark necessitated certain actions—like obtaining the blessing of the father-in-law, buying a ring, and devising a foolproof anti-denial proposal strategy.

Lia had unknowingly helped my efforts. By inviting me to spend part of the holidays with her family in Columbus, Ohio, she had basically handed me three days to accomplish the first task: convincing Rich, her father, that endorsing our union was in his firstborn daughter's best interest.

I really wanted to surprise Lia with my proposal. I believed there was a small window of opportunity in which to pull it off—just a few months' gap when she would not expect it, but would nevertheless say yes. I sensed that Lia and I were either currently in that window, or at least near it. So I figured if I could successfully check off the father's blessing without any funny stuff, my chances to astound her could only improve.

It seemed like a good plan. It probably was, except that I forgot to factor in human error—especially a human like me, with his heart in his throat and feathers sprouting from his elbows. Fortunately, my oversight did not cost me everything. But the price I paid will undoubtedly go down in matrimonial infamy.

I had had two previous encounters with Lia's family. The first time was during Lia's college graduation weekend. They had hosted a dinner for a gaggle of her friends, and I had led a game called Viking Master, which calls for hand motions and sound effects. Judging by their laughter, I figured I had made a good impression. However, Lia and I were not dating at the time, so her folks had not had their son-in-law antenna pricked, and sadly, my stellar actions slipped away like stars in a veil of overcast clouds.

The following Labor Day we drove up to Columbus, where I met Lia's parents for a second time. This time we were dating. The weekend was a blast: at dawn we ran with Lia's mother and her running buddies. Later, the whole family—Rich and Sue; Lia and I; and Lia's three siblings, Cara, Caitlin, and Chad—canoed down Blackhand Gorge in a veritable recreational watercraft armada. That evening,

I met Lia's grandparents, Ruth and Gus, and laughed at Ruth's reminiscences about Lia as a baby. It was about as packed and fun a weekend as I had ever had. When Lia and I packed to leave, Sue even hugged me. Rich shook my hand. By the time I got in the car, I was feeling pretty good about myself. Driving back and debriefing with Lia, I gleamed. All interaction had been constructive and positive. I had made them all laugh and had avoided saying anything stupid, and I even got the impression that they kind of liked me.

That was four months ago.

Lia had actually left for Columbus a few days before me. I had to wait for the weekend, so I was cruising to the Heartland solo, just me and my mind. But we were feeling courageous and optimistic. What was there to be afraid of? Lia and I were in love, and if her parents loved Lia, wouldn't they want her to be with the man she loved? Seemed logical to me. So as Mind and I drove by the Winston-Salem city limits, we hadn't a worry in the world.

We began a mental game we often play called Scenarios. It goes like this: I come up with a scenario, and my brain imagines what might happen. That's it. I guess some folks would just call it "thinking," but it is so fun, I like to call it a game.

In the present scenario, I was asking Rich if I could marry his daughter. To Mind, it all seemed so easy … *Let's see, at some point Rich will be bookbinding in the basement. He loves that. I'll pull away from Lia by saying, "Hmmm, I have to get a root beer from the fridge downstairs." Yes, that's good. And as I descend to the basement, I'll pretend I'm surprised to see Rich. I'll walk over as if inspecting, appear like I know what I'm doing, then ask him if there's anything I can … No, I'll ask him how I can help, and over a battered Hawthorne, I'll mention how honored—yes, honored—I am to be Lia's boyfriend. Is there a better word than boyfriend? I sound so young. I'll tell him … that I love his daughter, and that I'm going to marry her. Yeah, just lay it out there. He's a kind man, as far as I can see. Heck, how could he say no? I'm smart, funny, cute. I'm a stud!* This question-popping stuff would be a piece of cake.

So it seemed, until somewhere in the mountain mommas of West Virginia, the Scenarios game took a wrong turn. As I exited onto U.S. 33, my internal dialogue sounded slightly different.

At some point, Rich will challenge me to a game of hoops. I'll say sure. And while he's waxing me, he'll say something like, "So, Ned, what are your career aspirations?" I'll tell him that I'm enjoying working for the non-profit, but one day I want to be a writer. He'll ask, swishing a long-range jumper, "Have you published anything?" I'll tell him no. He'll ask, "Well, have you written anything yet?" I'll say not exactly. He'll say, "Sounds to me you're not a writer." I'll tell him he's right and proceed to look for a tree from which to hang myself. He'll say, "The Hawthorne tree behind the garage would be nice. It has a solid, low-hanging branch." It always came back to Hawthorne. I looked down to see if there was a scarlet "idiot" written across my chest. No, it was written across my forehead. *"Wait here while I fix you a noose," Rich would continue. "Learned how in Boy Scouts. I was an Eagle. Were you ever in the Boy Scouts, Ned? No? Shame. The Boy Scouts teach you to be prepared. That's their motto. It would have done you good to learn it."*

He was right. I was not prepared for this.

I was audibly clucking as I merged onto I-70 East into Columbus.

I decided to pray—more like make a deal with God: "Lord, if You want me to talk to Mr. Simpson, You need to give me a sign and present me with the perfect opportunity. If either or both fail to occur, I'll take it as Your divine providence that You want me to wait for Your will to be done at some later time (I sound so pious at times). Amen." As soon as I finished my prayer, I vowed to do everything in my power to avert my eyes from any approaching signs and to make sure the perfect opportunity never presented itself. Besides, signs were always open to interpretation, and all I had to do was stay by Lia's side in order to prevent any conversation with her father.

This was great! Realizing I could rationalize away even an answered prayer, I began to breathe easier. I was safe. I sighed in relief as I turned left onto Arlington Avenue, having thoroughly removed all faith from the equation. I had nothing to worry about.

The sign, clear as ink to paper, came Saturday.

Lia's grandparents took the grandkids (Lia, Cara, Caitlin, Chad, and me) out to lunch. Actually, they took us to a food court for lunch—or rather, handed us five dollars and told us to buy our own lunch. I followed Lia's sister Caitlin and bought a steak sandwich and fries while Lia walked over to a Taiwanese joint for some Pad Thai. We chomped and munched away, Lia forking her noodles (a cardinal sin in my book; Taiwanese food should only be eaten with chopsticks. *Once we're hitched, I'll convert her*, I thought. Five years later, Lia still utensilizes, and I've chalked that failure up alongside the others: refusing to drive stick shift, leaving a soggy sponge in the sink, and grinding her teeth while she sleeps).

We laughed as Gus and Ruth told stories meant to warmly embarrass their grandkids. Cara and Chad made fish lips, Caitlin showed us "the lazy eye," and Lia did the wave with her eyebrows. The only stupid trick I could claim was blowing my nose really loudly, but I decided to keep that to myself. Instead, I just sat back and laughed. I hadn't had this much fun in a food court since the days of straw-popping with a finger flick and breaking the bottoms of saltshakers with a coin and a fist—which wasn't that long ago.

This was a family I wouldn't mind joining, I thought.

At the end of the meal, Lia cracked open her fortune cookie and immediately turned red. She showed the paper to Ruth, whose gray hair bounced with delight, her eyes a Chinese fan of wrinkles. Lia's sisters and brother took a look and started to laugh. Gus proclaimed, "It's a sign!" Sign! Did Gus just say "sign"? What kind of sign was he talking about? Lia wouldn't let me read her fortune. I had that feeling one gets when he discovers he is the butt of everyone's joke. I got angry and turned violet.

Later that day, I finally twisted the fortune out of Lia's fist. It read, "The love of your life is before your very eyes." That I had been sitting directly across from her during lunch did not escape anyone's perception. Little as it was, it was a sign—the one I had been praying for, the one I was hoping God wouldn't give.

Heck, that was out of my control. A foreboding sensation made my knees feel weak as I realized the potential involvement of the supernatural. I reassured myself that the second part of my prayer—the part about the perfect opportunity—was something God had little power over. All I needed to do was not leave Lia's side. As long as I stayed glued to her hip, the situation could not present itself. Basically, I would be able to control my own destiny.

It's shocking when you realize how little control you actually have.

On Sunday, we celebrated Chad's good grades/birthday/Christmas by blindfolding him, piling into the family minivan, and driving to the east side of nowhere. On the way, Lia and her sisters sang while I laughed and hooted. It felt like we were going to summer camp at Lake Hockaloogie. For a second I thought we had stepped into *National Lampoon's Vacation* and were heading to Wally World; at one point I even thought I heard Sue lean over and call Rich "Clark."

We pulled into a driveway leading to a ranch-style house. It was a golden retriever puppy farm. Chad jumped for joy after we untied the bandana around his head and he realized where we were. He could choose any puppy he wanted. As we rushed to the gate, I encouraged Chad to take all the time he needed to make a wise decision. By my calculations, this family trip would consume most of the afternoon, and I could not foresee a time when I would be apart from Lia. One more evening, and I was golden.

The puppies were too young to take home but old enough to cuddle. Chad picked an amber one with a long snout and mellow demeanor. We spent the trip home thinking of dog names and slurping down A&W milkshakes.

As we pulled into the driveway, dusk was beginning to fall, and I inadvertently let my guard down for a millisecond. But that was all it took to let my wingwoman slip away.

Chad picked up a basketball, and we started a game of Around the World. I was hitting from long distance like Ray Allen, when one of Chad's buddies phoned. As he ran inside, I decided to hit one last shot before heading in—and that's when it happened.

I caught my rebound, tucked the ball underneath my arm, and turned for the door—and right into Mr. Simpson.

"Hey, Ned! You want to play a game of hoops?"

It was The Scenario!

"Uh, sure." What was I going to say—no?

"How about PIG?"

"You go first," I answered, bouncing him the basketball.

Rich took advantage, and soon I was at PI.

"So, do you and Lia have any big plans on the horizon?" Rich drained a free throw-distance jump shot.

He had asked the question!

If I had received an oracle message from Delphi, it would not have been any clearer. The perfect opportunity had arrived: basketball, no pressure, easy conversation—and he had made the first move.

Ned, if you don't go for it now, you're an idiot, I thought to myself.

"Nope, nothing out of the ordinary," I said.

Ned, what are you doing? That's not what you are supposed to say!
I accidentally hit a clutch shot to stay in the game.

"You and Lia have been dating for a while now …" Was that a question or a comment? He dinged his next shot off the rim.

"Oh, not long. We're just having a good time."

Not long? Good time? What was *that*?

I am ashamed of you, Ned, said my heart. *You are sad, weak, and pathetic. Let me out. I want a new body to inhabit.*

I banked in a shot, my back brushing bush branches, trying to conceal my yellow spine.

He bricked. Not sure if he did it on purpose.

"Well, we're glad you're here."

"Thanks," I said, wanting to leave.

I hit my next two shots for a come-from-behind win, shook Mr. Simpson's hand, and did not say another word. I had won PIG and lost my chance.

We didn't talk again until the most humiliating night of my life, which was still a month away.

Canvassing the sky for thunderclouds, I wondered if God still struck people down for blatant disobedience. In my mind's ear, I heard a distant rumble. I clucked inside all the way to Lia. I had done the dumbest thing I had ever done, and I would have to pay. Maybe what ensued was God's punishment or His sick sense of humor—or both.

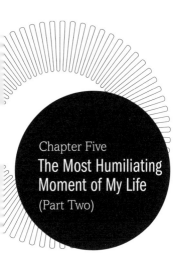

Chapter Five
The Most Humiliating Moment of My Life
(Part Two)

One thing that had made chickening out easier was that I knew I had another opportunity. Earlier that fall, Lia had asked if I would go with her to Columbus in January to watch some finger-skating show (I have been told the correct word is "figure" skating, but I refuse to believe it). Frankly, I'd rather slowly pick out my eyebrow hairs while watching paint dry than subject myself to three hours of leotards, axels, and salchows. But I said I'd go. You'll say yes to anything when you're in love, even to salchows.

So it was to be a finger-skating weekend. Lia's parents had bought the tickets, and I had a month to prepare myself for the showdown with Lia's father. Having witnessed my poultry inclinations, I knew this time I would need moral support—or the equivalent, a kick in the pants. Consequently, I asked several men who had gone through things of this nature before what they would do in my situation.

One encouraged me to call ahead, to give Rich a few days to prepare. He said, "Let the surprise occur when you are not in front of him. By the time you are finally face to face, he'll react better and have a ready answer." This had the ring of wisdom. I asked if this is what he had done.

"No way," he said. "I totally chickened out. I proposed first, and then went with Stacy to tell her parents." He shook his head. "Listen, don't do what I did; do what I say. Call first. Meet face to face. Do it right."

I decided to get a second opinion. I met with my friend Patrick and asked his opinion on the "call ahead of time" strategy.

He said, "Heck, yeah."

"Well, when?" I asked, caught slightly off-guard by his forthrightness.

"Tomorrow."

"Tomorrow?" I was about to lay an egg. "Can't I do it later in the week?"

"You call his butt tomorrow," he said.

I gulped, then asked if he had sought Jan's father's blessing.

"Sure did," he said. "But it was easy. He had Alzheimer's and said yes to everything. He didn't know who the heck he was talking to."

That was comforting.

The next day was Tuesday, January 18, 2000—the night Dan Blonsky won one million dollars on *Who Wants to Be a Millionaire?* Remember when everyone watched that show? Regis was interviewing Dan while my roommate, Sergio, and I watched from the couch. Pathetically, I was beginning to balk again. Portable phone in hand, I couldn't seem to muster the courage to dial the number.

Sergio counseled and coached me during Blonsky's early rounds.

"Well, does it feel right?"

"I don't know."

"If it feels right, do it. If it doesn't feel right, you're on drugs, 'cause Lia's awesome. So how does it feel?"

"It doesn't feel anything but scary ... I'm about to crap myself, Sergio. This is awful ... no, it's right." I tried to talk sense. "Sometimes you can't trust your feelings. After all, it's just a phone call to a nice guy."

"That's the spirit," said Sergio.

Commercial break.

"I'm doing it," I resolved. I got up and marched toward my bedroom. But as I passed the hall bathroom, a sudden rush of anxiety-adrenaline gripped my colon and a more pressing matter seized my attention. I sprinted to the can. Guess I really was about to crap myself.

Flushing, I heard Sergio announce that the commercial break was over.

Shoot.

Missed my chance, I thought. *Can't call during* Millionaire. *Everyone watches* Millionaire. *Don't want to disturb Rich from the pleasure of trivia with Regis Philbin.*

I returned to Dan Blonsky from Miami, Florida, a single lawyer who knew everything. I told Sergio that if Dan won the million, I'd take it as a sign. If not, I'd wait until tomorrow.

He shook his head at me.

The $500,000 question: whose face was on the first cover of *People* magazine in 1974? I don't think Dan Blonsky knew, but the friend he called, thanks to AT&T, said "Mia Farrow" without even first hearing the four multiple-choice options. How could you know something like that?

Sergio elbowed me in the ribs. "Down to the final question, buddy."

I braced myself. "Make it impossible, Regis!" I shouted at the television. The music crashed like lightning, making the tension rise.

"That music would freak out the Marlboro man," I said to Sergio. It was good of Regis to compose such music for his trivia show. Keep those Dan Blonsky brainiacs quaking in their loafers. Regis asked Dan, "What is the distance, in miles, between the earth and the sun? (A) 9.3 million, (B) 39 million, (C) 93 million, or (D) 193 million."

Dan, if you remember, started telling a story about astronomy class in college, sixteen years prior. He quickly knocked out options (A) and (D).

"Take the $500,000! Take the $500,000!" I cheered from my panic position on the living room couch. He looked to the ceiling; his head was moving like a man watching ping-pong. I think he was eenie-meenie-minie-moe-ing it! "Give up, DAN!" I screamed. "Go on, take the money and run!" He didn't. With an offhanded sigh, Dan said, "C, 93 million, final answer."

Dan Blonsky had done it. Cosmic momentum flowed from the New York studio southward into our brick house in North Carolina. I looked at Sergio, and he looked back at me. It was time.

Sergio smiled. "Ned, you better get on it. There's never been a better time than now."

I stomped straight to the bedroom, dialed the number, hit the OK button, and almost threw up. By the time the fiber-optic pulse connected Carolina to Ohio, all momentum had evaporated.

I still had my thumb on the OK button. A gentle depression would terminate the call, and I was about to push down when I heard a woman's voice on the other end of the line.

Mrs. Simpson! She was in her kitchen; I could tell. She had just turned off the faucet. I could picture her standing with her right hip leaning against the island, staring at the calendar containing her favorite pictures from last year. I wasn't in them.

I breathed into the phone.

She said "hello" a second time. I sensed she was about to place the earpiece back on the receiver. (Why didn't I let her?)

At that very moment, all rational thought departed, leaving sheer anarchy in my brain. The following internal monologue took less than a second (but it only takes a second to destroy your world): *A man is supposed to talk to the father, not the mother. I need to talk to Mr. Simpson, not Mrs. Simpson. At all costs, I must circumvent this interloper. I must devise a plan. Hmm. Aha! By Jove, I think I've got it! I'LL FAKE MY VOICE!*

Now, remember, I've lost my mind. I don't know why Mrs. Simpson seemed like such an obstacle. I don't know why I thought I couldn't talk to her, the mother, my future in-law. I know it sounds foolish. But at that moment, I wasn't thinking—at least not rationally. Please understand that I was under a terrible amount of stress, even though it was self-imposed. I was grasping for anything, and, unfortunately, my first thought was to fake my voice.

My voice came out sounding like a cross between Pee-wee Herman and Sylvester Stallone.

"Hello?" said Muffle Man (me). I was trembling on my mattress.

"Hello," Sue Simpson said for the third time, noticeably irritated.

"Uh, my name is Dr. Herman. I work for Wake Forest University … Medical School, and I would like to talk to … uh … Mr. Simpson."

Mrs. Simpson figured I must be asking for money. She decided to run interference: "He's busy. Can I take a message?"

"Uh, okay … no, wait, NO!" I raised my voice, and it cracked. "No, you will NOT take a message! I have a pressing matter I must discuss with Mr. Simpson. It is very important. It concerns his daughter." I started talking faster and squeakier: "I demand you get Mr. Simpson on the phone this instant!" I sounded like Mr. Jameson of the *Daily Bugle*, barking bad-breath orders at Peter Parker through my unlit cigar.

I must have come across harsh.

"Oh dear, Mr. Herman—that is your name, right?"

I grunted, my heart crawling up my throat. It had packed its bags and was trying to find the nearest exit, figuring that since my brain had already jumped ship, it was better to get out while it still could. This ship was going down.

"Well, I'm Sue Simpson, Lia's mother. You can talk to me."

"No!" I roared. "It is absolutely imperative that I speak to Mr. Richard Simpson. I cannot talk to you or anyone else about this. Do I make myself clear?" Did I just say what I think I did? Who *am* I? I'm lying to my future mother-in-law! Do I really think that after my conversation with Mr. Simpson, he's not going to go straight over to his wife and tell her everything we talked about?

"Okay, just a minute," she said. I heard her turn to someone beside her. Two feet scurried off, presumably to get Mr. Simpson.

I perceived breathing. She was staying on the line! What was I going to do now? Fake through a conversation with Mr. Simpson, too?

Hang up the phone! Hang up now*! You are ruining your life! Save yourself!*

But I couldn't. I couldn't do anything. I was paralyzed. I was done for. I was neck-deep in a hole I had dug for myself.

We breathed at each other like scuba divers sharing a mouthpiece.

Could she tell I was drowning?

I should have realized she was nervous herself. Who knows what was going through her mind? Had Lia gotten in trouble? Was she sick, hurt, dead? I could almost feel the pressure with which she was holding the phone to her ear.

From somewhere inside, I heard a voice: *Come clean. Come clean, Ned.* The voice echoed in my cranial vacancy. *Come clean.* The resonance made my head ache.

Maybe if I obey, it will shut up, I thought.

So I whispered, "Mrs. Simpson ... Mrs. Simpson!"

The sudden switch in voice scared her. I realized my whisper was more of a rasp—a rather good ghost impersonation, as I recall.

"Yes!" She jumped, startled.

"It's ... it's Ned." I continued to whisper, tears filling my eyes and snot filling my nose.

"Ned, what are you doing?"

"I don't know." Probably the most honest thing I have ever said in my life. "I just need to talk to Mr. Simpson. I'm stupid."

"Well, all right. Hold on. I'll get him," she said in a mom voice. She had regained her calm. She placed the receiver on the island and found Rich.

In the meantime, I fought for composure.

Mr. Simpson's voice came through. "Hello?" He sounded confused, probably because of the look on his wife's face.

"Mr. Simpson." I lapsed into Pee-wee/Stallone but quickly returned to my natural voice, which was not entirely natural anymore, due to the crying, stress, and brainlessness: "I'm looking forward to seeing you this weekend."

"Good. We're looking forward to seeing you, too," he answered cautiously, judiciously.

"Um … uh …" I was fumbling again. I almost clucked! "I was wondering if we could find some time to talk."

"Sure, we can go for a run or get some coffee."

"The only thing is that Lia cannot know."

"Oh! Okay. Well, we'll figure it out."

"Thanks." I almost hung up. I should have. Instead, I held on in a silent stupor.

"So, is that it?" Mr. Simpson said in the awkward void.

I was filled with guilt and anguish. Stupidly, I said, "Um, could I talk to Mrs. Simpson one last time?" What was I thinking? Hadn't I made things bad enough?

"Sure," said Rich, handing his wife the phone.

She got back on.

"Mrs. Simpson. Oh, Mrs. Simpson," I spouted in a flourish. "I'm so sorry about lying to you. I'm so sorry about everything. I promise I'll never call or pretend I'm Dr. Herman or pretend I'm anything else I'm not. I just needed to talk to Mr. Simpson, and I didn't know what to do when you got on. Well, I know it doesn't make sense. I mean, it's not a secret; you need to know, too. Oh! But

Lia's not allowed! I mean, Lia isn't allowed to know. So, bye now."

I pressed the OK button. Long overdue. The phone went dead. I went limp. I don't think I gave Mrs. Simpson a chance to speak. I'm pretty sure I hung up on her.

I ran over to Sergio and told him what had happened; he hyperventilated at my expense.

It was Tuesday. I had three days to kill myself. Three days to fake a knee injury. Three days to figure out a way to wiggle out of finger skating. Three days before facing Mr. Simpson, and I had already managed to make it the worst experience of my life.

The doorknob turned. Sergio and I jerked our attention to the door. It was Lia. I quickly passed a don't-say-a-word look to my roommate, and we both stifled laughter.

Lia stayed only an hour or so—for some reason, I seemed preoccupied. She left annoyed.

Before bed, toothbrush and foam in mouth, I looked at myself in the mirror.

"Hello," I said to my reflection. "My name's Butthead. What's yours?"

Believe it or not, I didn't commit suicide. Instead, I decided to let the Simpsons kill me in Columbus.

On Friday, I was an hour late picking up Lia. I had been ring shopping and had lost track of time—a worthy excuse, but one I could not use. So, hedging my bets, I lied and told her I had gotten stuck at the office. The result was a chilled silence all the way to West Virginia, something I actually welcomed. I think if I had opened my mouth, I would have been sick.

Once we hit farmland, I started to apologize. I confessed in generalities, and eventually she warmed up or cooled down or whatever she needed to do to equilibrate.

We pulled into the circle driveway of Lia's house around midnight. Rich had long fallen asleep. Sue and I exchanged a couple of knowing looks.

When Lia was out of earshot, I whispered, "Sorry again about the phone call."

Sue laughed, cradling little Millie, Chad's puppy, in her arms.

"I'm sorry you were there to witness the most humiliating moment of my life."

She chuckled. "What were you thinking?" she asked.

I didn't give an answer because I didn't have one.

Lia walked back in the room, and we changed the subject as we all headed for bed. I knew bed that night was a formality for me; I would find no rest in a pillow and sheets. I nestled my head in my interlaced fingers and stared in the direction of a ceiling I could not see. I think I dozed at some point in the wee hours because I don't remember the sunrise.

By the time I dressed, brushed my teeth, and went downstairs, Lia was still snoozing, but Rich was gone. I didn't see either of them until lunchtime when we sat around the kitchen island, the setting of Tuesday's catastrophe. Rich was slurping soup and munching grilled cheese. I caught myself staring at his forehead; he sure was taking his time with things. Saturday was slipping away; I could feel its departure like quicksand under my feet. Had Rich forgotten about our conversation? What was he waiting for? Was he stalling because the news he was planning to give wasn't the good kind? Or was he waiting for me to make the first move?

It didn't occur to me that he might be nervous also. Lia was his eldest daughter; he, too, was new at this. The situation wasn't easy for either of us.

As we finished sliding the final morsels of lunch down our throats on the brown fizz of Coca-Cola, one of the girls suggested we head to the downtown athletic club for the afternoon and work off some calories in preparation for the night's finger-skating show.

Sounded like a good idea to everybody. The Simpsons like to do things together.

We put our dishes in the washer, and everyone went off to their quarters to assemble their workout gear. Because it was winter, I hadn't thought to pack any shorts. I told Lia this as we walked upstairs together.

"Don't worry," she said, "I'm sure my dad has a pair you can borrow."

He did, and I wondered if my life could get any more awkward. In a few minutes, we were all bundling up by the door.

The Athletic Club of Columbus is a beautiful, hundred-year-old building with mahogany, marble, and plush everything. It is grand and austere and first-class and imposing, especially to a bumpkin like me. I was amazed to discover a pool on the fourth floor and a basketball court on the top floor. The ACC can accommodate fancy parties in its ballrooms and gourmet dining in its own restaurant. It has a grill on the sixth floor with great bean-and-bacon soup. I'm pretty sure some guys even sleep there. And why not? This building has everything you could ask for.

We spun through the turnstile thumps of the entrance and found ourselves face to face with a life-sized picture. It was so big I had to step back to adjust my eyes. At once, I discovered that the image was none other than my future father-in-law. He was the president! I struggled to keep my jaw from dropping.

In an instant, a whirlwind of welcomes descended upon us like a chorus of Hallelujah angels: "Hello, Mr. Simpson." "How are you today, Mr. Simpson?" "This must be your family, Mr. Simpson." "Can I carry your bag, Mr. Simpson?"

Rich smiled and introduced us all. He called me "Lia's friend, Ned." We walked through the barrage of cordiality onto an elevator that carried us to locker rooms. I felt small.

The locker room was an obstacle course of fat, naked old men with towels draped on their shoulders instead of cinched around their bellies. It was sick. I couldn't stop staring.

Every locker had a name plate. Rich's said "President 2000." There was a sink nearby with free razors, combs, aftershave lotion, and blue smelly water whose purpose eluded me.

I decided to stick with Chad and just do what he did, hoping that no one, least of all Mr. Simpson, would recognize how out of my element I was. But Chad was too slick and speedy, and he was out the door before I had my jacket off.

The next thing I knew, I was alone with Mr. Simpson, who was down to his skivvies and showing off his chiseled fifty-year-old physique.

Gulp.

I stripped down to my boxers and did my best gut-suck.

Rich moved from one leg to the other. He looked like John Wayne, without the hat and the clothes.

"So, Ned, that thing you wanted to talk about—is it something we could discuss here, or will it require more time?"

I shifted. Invisible spurs clicked into the carpet. High noon in Silverado. It was the moment of truth. It was showdown. No turning back.

I took in a sharp, steady breath. Was I ready for this? No. But I was finished with the waiting. It was now or never.

Rich straddled a lacquered bench like it was his steed; I sauntered up next to him.

He looked me in the eyes.

I looked back into his and said, "Well, the length of the conversation depends on you, I suppose." Pause. "You probably have a good idea what I'd like to talk about."

"I think I have a pretty good idea," he said.

We were gun-slinging, and it was time to draw.

"Mr. Simpson, I'd like to marry Lia." I allowed a second to pass. "And before I propose, I would like to have your blessing."

There it was. Sheriff Simpson and Little Neddy the Kid squared off in our underwear, imaginary tumbleweed blowing across our path, barbecued beef brisket wafting from Rex's grill back at the Double B Ranch.

He let the moment linger; with twiddling fingers he tickled the trigger at his side. I knew he knew and he knew I knew that he had my heart in his hand.

The sensation was not a pleasant one.

He gave a wry smile, and finally said, "Sue and I are more than excited about you marrying our daughter. We think you are great for each other. If you want to wait a couple of years, or one, or get married this summer, just give us the word, and we'll be excited to celebrate alongside you. We can't wait for you to become a part of our family."

He looked relieved.

I certainly was. I would have hugged him, had it not been for the fact that we were practically naked.

Outside, Lia wondered what was taking us so long.

We kept our mouths shut.

———

So there it is. The worst and, consequently, one of the best experiences of my life, on paper for all to read. Lia, I hope you are happy. And I guess I can finally laugh about it, too.

Chapter Six
Engagement

Engagement is not flying; it is not falling. It is awkward suspension, a dangling in space.

Engagement is a car trip where the next rest area is in forty-one miles and your bladder is about to explode.

Engagement is relational purgatory. It is not hell, and it certainly is not heaven. It is that space in between. And there is still work to be done.

Engagement is our life—or a lot like our life. It is a microcosmic time. It is the steady ticking of a clock, the even marching of a boot, a long journey from birth to an ever-larger, looming death of sorts. Hoping there is an afterlife.

Engagement is a longing; it is a promise and waiting—the promise of something better, the waiting for it to come.

Engagement is the introduction to life for, God willing, the next half-century, and at the same time, a crash course in a million things you'll never need to know again.

Engagement is in-law formalities and money and a thousand decisions that seemingly have no meaning. It is learning the four Cs. It is learning new words like *votive* and *topiary*.

Engagement is tracking down groomsmen and getting their suit sizes, which of course they don't know.

Engagement is parting with your bachelor-pad furniture. It is finding out that your wife does not want your *Blues Brothers* poster hanging in the living room.

Come to think of it, engagement is a lot like being 106 miles from Chicago with a full tank of gas and half a pack of cigarettes, when it's dark and you're wearing sunglasses, as Elwood says in the movie.

Engagement is learning there are a million flowers with a million fruity names, and you can buy them all for a hundred million dollars.

Engagement is getting physically sick after you discover the cost of a ceremony and reception.

Engagement is cake-tasting and frosting-sampling until you overdose.

Engagement is using "the gun" (the greatest invention conceived to date to occupy men while shopping) in stores you have never set foot in, like Williams-Sonoma, Pottery Barn, and Bed Bath & Beyond.

Engagement is the realization that you don't have anyone's address and that it takes six sheets of paper, three envelopes, and two stamps to send an invitation to your current roommate.

Engagement is telling and retelling and retelling yet again the same proposal story and making it sound like it's the first time you've ever told it.

Engagement is needing a five- and ten-year plan (and discovering that anything you say will do, as long as you state it with confidence).

Engagement is realizing that lots of people care, that lots of people love you, and that you can't invite them all.

Engagement is finding out that premarital counseling is actually helpful, and that help is exactly what you will need to get through all of this.

Engagement is getting advice. It is as if you are wearing a sign that says, "Advise me." You get inundated with marital counsel, whether you ask for it or not. Anyone who is married has some to give, like little Confucian-sounding nuptial proverbs that make no sense whatsoever:

"Marriage is great, and marriage is hard."

"Marriage is not the Promised Land."

"Marriage is a covenant, not a contract."

Thanks for the definitions, I'd want to say.

Other friends would give more tangible but no less senseless instruction, such as:

"Don't turn the lights off angry."

So I should smile as I do it? I would think.

Another friend told me, "Sometimes the most loving thing to say is nothing."

I could picture holding Lia and having her ask me to say something romantic. I would draw her close and say, "Nothing." Lia would love that.

A girl told us, "Never eat in front of the television."

That is going to be tough; there's not much room behind it.

Clearly, I was not ready for this. But the more advice I received, the more I realized that people didn't know what they were talking about. Or, at least nothing was universal. We were advised:

"Get a pet."

"Don't get a pet."

"Get a plant."

"Give each other chores."

"Get a maid."

"Work out your own problems."

"Put your counselor on speed dial."

"Plan surprises for each other."

"Talk about everything."

I'd say okay and proceed to forget what they had said.

Some friends just wanted to give us the "keys." Marriage seemed to have a lot of them. We learned:

"Communication is the key."

"Kindness is the key."

"Unconditional love is the key."

"Friendship is the key."

"Sticking to a budget is the key."

"Giving your wife an allowance is the key."

We laughed as we pictured the size of the key ring we were going to need.

Lia and I received so much advice. We're sure it was all well-meaning. It was just too much to process. In the end, I decided to cling to my two favorites—one for its simplicity, the other for its absurdity.

My pastor told me the first. "Follow this one equation, and you'll be fine: Happy Wife = Happy Life."

Now, that's advice. That seemed easy enough. As long as I kept Lia happy, everything would be wonderful. How little I knew about marriage.

The second was given to me by an elderly woman. She told me, "When you fight, fight naked." That seemed fun (and believe it or not, it works).

I confess we threw out most of the advice we received as if it were junk mail, but we have found since that most of it was valuable.

That was long after the engagement was over.

Engagement is an overwhelming wave that churns you up and spits you out.

Engagement is a moment when it all hits: things are a lot bigger than you. You are a small cog in life's grand wheel. You are just a pawn dressed in penguin getup.

And yet it is a moment when you absolutely know you have a role—you are a cast member; you play a part in this drama. You even have lines (of course, they do not trust you with them; instead, you get them spoon-fed to you by a robed guy who is reading them out of a script).

Engagement is the *click, click, click* of a steadily rising coaster. It is anticipation. It is stress. It is wondering when and if it will ever end.

And before you know it and before you're ready, it does. One final *click*, and you crest the hill; you can barely see the bottom. You're buckled in, and there's no turning back.

And you are swept up in the sudden rush of a wedding-weekend free fall. And it flies by in a blur. And is gone.

You get seeds or bubbles blown at you. You jump in your car. You have never heard or felt a car so quiet. So you turn the ignition and turn to your wife, hoping the first will fire and the second will reassure.

And you drive away. And you want to cry. But you're not sure why.

And you're struck with how nothing has prepared you for this moment or the rest.

And your new wife feels the same.

So you hold hands.

And together you drive into the night, wishing you had brighter headlights, wishing you could see farther into the future than your hood, hoping the directions you pulled off the Internet will get you where you need to go, and wondering why what's ahead smells so fishy ...

... Then three days later, finding the dead mackerel your groomsmen duct-taped to your front fender.

Chapter Seven

The Beauty Battle

In 1963 Jimmy Soul gave the airwaves, and the people listening, some marital advice: "If you wanna be happy for the rest of your life, never make a pretty woman your wife. So from my personal point of view, get an ugly girl to marry you."[1]

Lia assures me these are the correct lyrics. To me, it sounds like he sings, "If you wanna be happy for the rest of your life, never make a pygmy woman your wife"—which makes sense. Who wants to marry a pygmy ... except a pygmy? But as usual, Lia is right. If only I had known earlier ... I married a pretty one.

But she wasn't always that way—pretty, that is. At least, that's the way her grandparents remember it. They told me so that first Labor Day weekend-o-fun I spent with Lia's family. In the morning, we had jogged with Sue and her running buddies, you recall; in the afternoon, we had paddled down Blackhand Gorge in our recreational watercraft armada; and in the evening, we had had Lia's grandparents, Gus and Ruth, over for dinner.

Gus, a veteran from the Second World War and retired CIA employee, had a slick-back to his hair and a tough-as-nails grit to his eyeballs. And when he laid those eyeballs on me that evening, I felt a fear I had never experienced before. Sweating in trepidation, I watched his mouth draw back and expose his teeth. There was no telling whether Gus was grinning or growling, and I expected the worst. And before I was ready, he grabbed my hand, his vice-grip squeezing every ounce of blood out of it. He leaned in and tightened the hold. With my free hand I grasped the table beside me, for my knees had buckled under the pressure. I was instantly at his mercy, and I think he knew it.

Ruth greeted me next. I moved toward her, extending my limp hand in her direction. But Ruth would have none of that; she bypassed my hand with a wave and swung both her arms around my neck. She held me vigorously. Then, partly withdrawing, she kept a grip on my shoulders and gave my face a measured look, contemplating, as if she were leveling a picture frame. Needless to say, I hung on her approval, which thankfully came in an instant: "What a handsome young man!" Ruth looked back and forth between Lia and me; her small face beamed with delight. "What a looker!"

Oh boy, the Simpsons sure are going to get a kick out of that. I tried to smile while I silently prayed that my sunburn might conceal the blush. I knew I was at her mercy, too.

"You should have seen Lia when she was born," Ruth reminisced with a coquettish sigh. "She was so hairy, I thought her mom had given birth to a gorilla."

"Ruth!" chided Sue, Lia's mom.

"Remember? We used to call her 'monkey girl.' Do you remember that, Lia?"

All of a sudden, Lia was the one turning red.

This is more like it, I thought. Someone else was in the hot seat. Lia laughed, hoping to conceal her mortification in her giggles, but it was like trying to hide a glowing stick of uranium in your pocket. We all saw it.

Except Ruth, who kept going: "We used to say, 'Who's our

monkey girl?' and Lia would start the monkey dance ..." Ruth demonstrated, putting her right hand to her head and her left to her armpit. She shaped her lips into a ring, hooted monkey noises, and started bouncing from one leg to the other.

Lia looked over to the sink and calculated the possibility of disappearing down the disposal, never to return.

"That's enough," said Sue, but she was laughing. Everyone was, including me. Ruth was hysterical.

"You think that all babies are cute when they're born," Ruth continued, "but not Lia. She was ug-ly. I've never seen so much hair. Fortunately, most of it fell off ... eventually."

Poor Lia was purple with embarrassment.

And all of a sudden, I understood a little better.

I had always wondered why Lia underplayed her beauty, why she kept her hair obscured in a ponytail, hid in baggy clothes, dismissed my "you look cute" comments. I had been perplexed. Why would a girl veil her beauty? But then I realized what was going on: Lia didn't believe she was attractive. And how could she? Growing up, she was called a primate!

She was monkey girl. She was not human. As the rest of mankind evolved, somehow natural selection had left her behind. Sure, her family didn't mean it, but their teasing did the teaching. Subtle as it was, Lia learned to believe she would never be like the others, that she would always be overlooked—that, fight as she might, she would always lose the battle for beauty. She was not beautiful—to her, it was cold, hard truth. And never once did she doubt their opinion; never once did she question her conviction.

That reminds me of what Mitya says to Alyosha in *The Brothers Karamazov*: "The awful thing is that beauty is mysterious as well as terrible. God and the devil are fighting there and the battlefield is the heart of man."[2] The awful part was that the beauty battle had left a mark. By the time Lia came into my life, her self-image was battle-worn and battle-broken; God and the devil had been fighting there, and the devil seemed to be winning. As a result, when Lia looked in the mirror, she saw a terrible thing, something worse than ugliness: she saw something boring, a normal face and a normal figure that would attract the attention of no one.

Dense and dumb as a rock, I had always thought Lia was just being modest when she covered up her knockout body in oversized sweaters. Really, she thought that there was nothing to see.

Beauty is a mystery. What makes one person beautiful and another person not? What is it about the angle of a nose, the fullness of a lip, the curl of a lash that stirs a man's heart? What is it about the gleam of an eye, the curve of a hip, the size of a breast that stirs a man's groin? What is it? Confucius is quoted as saying, "Everything has its beauty, but not everyone sees it."[3] Well, that's a nice sentiment, but when you're the ugly duckling, it offers little consolation. When others tell you that you are not beautiful, whether with words or with the absence of words, beauty becomes a terrible thing—and Lia, like many girls, had never heard the words "you are beautiful." Oh, they might have been uttered, and certainly they were meant, but just because words are spoken does not mean they are heard. That is a different experience.

At least, that's what I learned in premarital counseling, which Lia and I both loved—until Alan, the pastor, pulled out his invisible skeleton key and picked the locks on the secret door to our hearts. Who loves having their stuff sifted through? Not me. In my expert opinion, it is much better to hide anything that might cause pain.

My old bachelor apartment taught me that if you let the dust settle, you can hardly tell there's dirt. It is only after you kick it up that breathing becomes difficult.

On top of that, sharing your secrets with some third party who speaks from a pulpit seemed mighty risky to me. I mean, when he started preaching about how sinful we were and how much we needed a Savior, it was kind of scary to think that he might actually be speaking about us.

"A little pain now will save a lot of pain later," answered Alan, when I asked him during a session why we had to go through this. "Trust me. We won't have any earthquakes ..."

... *Unless we discover a fault line*, I could tell he was thinking.

And sure enough, he found one.

The eruption occurred at our third meeting. Up to that point, our sessions had been somewhat fun; we had taken personality tests, talked about things we had in common, and shared our hopes for the future. Today our topic was family history, which didn't seem too dangerous. However, when Alan asked Lia to share about the first time she heard she was beautiful, I felt the tremors.

When Lia cries, it comes out of every opening: tear ducts, nostrils, mouth. It's disgusting, and I could sense lava flow perking the moment Alan opened his mouth.

I actually heard it before I saw it. It sounded like a tornado-warning siren. Then I felt the earth quake, and the sensation sent me shuddering. I gulped and braced myself before peeking over at my bride-to-be.

She did not look good.

Instantly, I blamed Alan. I looked back and stared at him. With my eyes I yelled, *See, now look what you've done!*

Alan didn't seem to sense my telepathy. He was focused on my fiancée. Scooching to the edge of his stuffed chair, he asked, "Has anyone ever told you that you're beautiful?"

Lia's wet face was in her hands. She shook her head sideways, and water seeped through her fingers.

"Lie!" I shouted. "I'm sure I've told her a hundred times!"

Lia shook her head.

"Sure, I have. She must have that selective-hearing deficiency or something." I turned to Alan and caught him smiling; he seemed to be relishing the exchange. "*You've* heard me say it, haven't you?" I looked at both of them. "Well, maybe not in words, but certainly in action. I hold her hand and stuff. Why would I marry someone I didn't think was beautiful? What am I, stupid?"

Alan didn't answer.

Lia cried louder.

I got nervous. *Maybe I haven't ever said it. I think I have, but it's not one of those lines that naturally comes out in conversation. Well, no time like the present.* "Lia, you're beautiful," I said. "There, is that better?"

It wasn't.

I put my arm around her shoulder and squeezed.

She recoiled.

Thanks a lot, Alan, I said with angry eyes. *I thought marriage counseling was supposed to teach me how to avoid situations like this. What's the big deal anyway? No one has ever told me I'm beautiful, and I'm all right.*

I was feeling that feeling I least like to feel: out of control.

I threw my hands up as if to say to Alan, *Looks like we've got a crying girl on our hands. I've done my best; now it's your turn. After all, you're the one who got us in this mess in the first place!*

Alan answered my gaze with a question: "Ned, what does your fiancée need right now?"

"Don't ask me. She was fine until you started talking," I answered, a little too strongly.

Alan graciously disregarded my harangue. "No, what does she need from you?"

"Um ... I don't know. I've tried the talk-real-sweet technique and the pat-on-the-back technique. I'm out of ideas."

Was it getting hot in here? It sure felt like it. Alan's eyes had shifted fully from her to me; Lia's sobs subsided as she sensed the attention leaving her.

"Ned, she needs you to understand."

"Understand what?" Sometimes I'm denser than petrified wood.

"What she's feeling. What is Lia feeling?" His question made me feel like a second-grader.

"She's feeling ... upset?" I ventured.

Alan nodded.

"Lia is upset," I said more confidently. "So, how do I fix it?"

"It's not about fixing; it's about listening and trying to understand. You're right; Lia is upset. What else?"

Lia nodded agreement.

"Err ... she feels ugly? But she's wrong."

"I know that, and you know that, but feelings aren't wrong. What she feels is real; she wants you to understand what she is feeling. She doesn't want you to fix her, just to listen to her with compassion."

Listen?

Ugh. I looked over to my fiancée. She definitely wasn't beautiful now: puffy eyes, purple face, gooey junk coagulating above her upper lip.

I opened my mouth but had no clue what to say. Beseechingly, I looked back at our pastor for help.

He let me squirm a bit longer, but he understood—after all, he's a man. Once upon a time, he was an idiot just like me.

Alan handed Lia a Kleenex.

Should have thought of that.

He moved from his chair and knelt beside her. He rested his hand on her ponytail and prayed.

Lia's face started returning to normal.

"Ned, I want you to do what I do, and say what I say."

Now I knew Alan was treating me like a second-grader. He was playing Follow the Leader, and there was nothing to do but play along.

So, coaching me line by line and motion by motion, Alan slowly patched things up enough to sustain our engagement—at least until our next meeting.

He watched us leave, shaking his head, knowing I was going to have to learn things the hard way.

I lied a few lines ago. True, no one has ever told me I'm beautiful, but I'm *not* okay with it. The truth is, I am an ugly duckling—and I'm not changing into a swan. I don't see beauty in the mirror; I see blemish. I see things I wish I could change but cannot. I'm too short. I have thick red hair and freckles that splotch. I get zits in the wrong places at the wrong times. And I've got the biggest bubble butt you've ever laid eyes on. I am an ugly freak of nature.

We never measure up, do we? We all have secret and not-so-secret characteristics we hate about ourselves. There is no one who is beautiful to himself or herself.

And buried in that insecurity is the inability to believe that anyone else feels the way you do. Everyone else seems to have it all together, and you are the only one with a justifiable complex.

The awful thing is that beauty is mysterious as well as terrible. God and the devil are fighting there, and the battlefield is the heart of man. A war is raging inside all of our hearts. One side is truth, the other side a lie. One sees reality, the other a distortion. One says, "You are the apple of my eye"; the other says, "You are monkey girl" or "carrot top" or "bubble butt." God and the devil have been fighting on the battlefield of Lia's heart for twenty-seven years, ever since she came out looking like a gorilla. I bet to God she came out looking like an angel.

Lia called this last Valentine's Day "lame." That's what she said as I called her, coming home late from work, having told her that I had made no reservations for dinner and confessing that my card, which for a twist I had decided to mail, hadn't yet arrived. All I had was a rock and an icy wife who didn't want to be with me.

I fixed spaghetti because it is the meal I make when I haven't spent any time thinking about what to make, and we ate in silence because Lia knows that I hate silence.

Like I said, all I had was a rock, so after washing the tomato sauce off the dishes, I pulled it out of my bag and tossed it her direction.

"What's this?" Lia said sardonically.

"It's a rock," I replied.

"Thanks." Her sarcasm was loud and clear.

This was going to bomb; I could feel it.

I approached her with trepidation. "It's a geode," I said.

She rotated the stone with her fingers.

Here goes nothing, I said to myself. *Better to crash and burn than stay cooped up on the tarmac.*

What are you talking about? It's better to stay on the tarmac, bonehead, I answered myself.

Maybe you're right, I agreed. *But this night might be an exception because as far as it looks, you are already dead.*

I took a deep breath and sighed.

Lia was an arm's length away. I reached over, touched her cheek, and stroked her hair. I said, "Sometimes what we see isn't what's really there. This looks like a rock, but in reality it's a precious stone. Sometimes when you look in the mirror, you think you see a rock, but you are not seeing the whole picture. You are not seeing what I see. You are not seeing what God sees. You are not seeing what is really there. Lia, I love you. To me, you are the most beautiful woman in the whole world—not just on the inside, but the whole deal. You turn me on, and you warm my heart. You are the most precious treasure. You are my greatest gift. You are the love of my life. It's time to break it open. It's time to break through."

As I talked, I witnessed the ice melting.

I took her hand and led her to the basement. I pulled a hammer from my toolbox, and we smashed the geode together. It was a glorious catharsis. Our heads touched as we admired the pieces. The inside was a creamy blue, like peering into a cave made of ocean and clouds. I was struck by how it paled in comparison to the beauty breathing beside me.

If you want to be happy for the rest of your life, marry a woman who does not believe she is beautiful, and watch Love win the battle.

For a moment, with a hammer, we broke it open. There was a breakthrough, a break in the battle, and we saw things clearly ... but we'd be fools to believe that the war is over.

The beauty battle is not won with a single marriage consultation or a geode on a lame Valentine's Day. Lia will still struggle with the picture she has of herself, and I will still struggle with mine. There are more lies we will listen to, more troops on the horizon, and more pain to inflict on others and on ourselves.

But it will not last forever. One day, the war will cease. One day, good will finally triumph. One day, I believe we will break through for good. And on that glorious day, truth will set us free; truth will reign supreme. And we will know the beauty we always were, the beauty we truly are, and the beauty we always will be. May the day come soon.

Chapter Eight
Gifts

"Buying a gift," Gary said, "is like naming a kid: everything you think of will be interpreted the wrong way."

"What do you mean?" I asked. I dipped the pointy end of a tortilla chip into salsa and listened.

"Say you name your kid 'Dave,'" Gary explained. "You think the name is solid, safe, satisfactory. You love little Davey, and the kids like him at preschool. Everything seems fine until the first day of kindergarten, when some butthead says that Dave lives in a grave and starts making ghost noises. All the kids laugh. Little Gravy Davey starts to cry, and then Butthead says 'boo-hoo,' and everyone howls, and your son is scarred for life. The next thing you know, Dave becomes a mute, starts drawing pictures of people without appendages, and only wears black. Your only option is to homeschool him, send him to a therapist, and remove all the sharp objects from the house."

"Wow, you have really thought this through," I said.

I was pondering all this when a sudden flashback rushed into my mind: rustling leaves, a fall day, and a chanting yellow school bus ... *Redhead Ned in bed with Ted. He hit his head and now is dead!* (I could have strangled Dr. Seuss.) I shook my redhead Ned head and told Gary I understood. "But what did the kids call you?" I asked.

Scratching his two-day stubble, he lamented, "Change the G to an F, and you'll know the reason why the only date I could get to prom was a guy named Ralph."

"Those jerks," I said.

"So, presents," said Gary, returning to the subject, "are a lot like that: whatever you wrap can and will be received the wrong way."

Gary had been dating Kate for nearly a year. He really liked her, but with an anniversary coming up, he was lost as to what to get her. Here was Gary's problem: if he gave her something expensive such as jewelry, he would set the bar too high, an unmatchable precedent that would either drain his bank account or cause all future gift exchanges to end in disappointment. On the other hand, if he handed her a signed Hallmark over dinner at Fast Food Eddies, he may have compromised future anniversaries and would appear, heaven forbid, cheap. Hence, he was leaning toward a spa gift certificate. It seemed perfect. Let a professional do the pampering for you. It was like sending in a pinch hitter, like calling in the ace reliever, like hiring an escort service to show your lady a good time ... because you couldn't. Somehow, it didn't sound so perfect anymore.

Fairy Gary was in quite a pickle, a dilemma in which we men find ourselves at least four times a year—the Big Four, I call them: (1) the anniversary, (2) the birthday, (3) Christmas, and (4) Valentine's Day (the most evil holiday of them all—a day conceived by evil women in order to satisfy three guilty pleasures at once: flowers, chocolate, and foot massages).

Poor guy, I could see his conundrum. If he didn't decipher the gift riddle, he could kiss a great year and a great gal goodbye.

I said with a sigh, "I wish I were more help, but I have never succeeded with Lia."

"What do you mean? You're married, aren't you? Obviously something worked," Gary pointed out.

I shook my head, put a hand on his shoulder, and said with a wry smile, "No, it's because of the skeleton suit."

Lia and I had been dating for two months. Things were going great. We were veritably in love. When September 24 rolled around, we celebrated my birthday.

Now, for me growing up, birthdays did not attract much hoopla, which was actually the way I liked it. At most, I received a card or two, a couple of presents, and an ice cream cake. My idea of a surprise was trick candles. (I really liked them.) I never wanted the big party thing. My dad was the same way. Even during the elementary years, we never did the clown or the roller rink or the petting zoo or Chuck E. Cheese's. Birthdays were simply not a big deal.

Every year or so, my mom would wrap her arms around my shoulders and ask if I wanted a party. I would say, "Thanks, but no thanks. Just get me a present or two and an ice cream cake with trick candles." She would say okay and sound disappointed.

See, I was a shy kid; I just hid it by being extroverted. As outgoing as I appeared, I had a shy streak as straight and long as the Mason-Dixon Line. The mere suggestion of a birthday party felt like going to the dentist's office. However, to Lia and the Simpsons, birthdays were holidays. Birthdays were when your wildest dreams came true. Birthdays needed pony rides and themes and chocolate medallions wrapped in gold. Birthdays needed a celebration.

Since Lia and I have been together, I have come to see things from her perspective, at least in theory. Birthdays are special, or should be. It is the one day we commemorate a particular person, a particular life. It is the most other-centered celebration, the most generous of events; it is on birthdays, and birthdays alone, that we give without expecting in return. It is the ultimate holiday of appreciation and should be celebrated with zest and zeal.

Come to think of it, I actually have no problem celebrating for a friend. But in return, I'd rather experience something milder. If you feel the impulse to get me something, just give me a card, a practical gift, an ice cream cake with trick candles, and a quiet night at home.

Back to September 24. This was our first holiday as a couple, and since Lia is the kind of girl who listens, she did a wonderful job. We cooked spaghetti together at my house. She buttered a loaf of Italian bread and sprinkled some garlic salt in the notches. I stirred noodles with my left hand and tomato sauce with my right. Lia made some pink lemonade and put our plates on place mats she had brought from home. I commented that we were a good team.

As we ate, I unearthed a particularly long string of pasta and placed an end between Lia's lips. Placing the other in mine, we impersonated Lady and the Tramp, trying to keep a straight face. Lia dabbed my chin with her napkin to collect an errant glob of sauce. I talked about summers on my grandparents' ranch, riding horses and getting chiggers. Lia said that she would love to visit it one day. I cleared the table, and Lia lit candles on top of a generic, store-bought ice cream cake. I blew until I felt my eyes begin to roll back into my head. But those trick candles kept coming back. Eventually, I became bored and extinguished the fire with wet fingers.

She handed me a card, which I read thoughtfully. I don't remember what it said—probably something sentimental and sweet. I thanked her, and we segued to the living room, where she handed me a wrapped thing I could only assume was my present.

I took it from her and did the mandatory shake test. The wrapping paper was wrinkled and colorful, covering something soft and plastic. I surveyed the side, looking for flaps to rip. Soon corners peeked through. I was taking my time.

Unbeknownst to me, Lia's heart was beating in vivace tempo. To her, this gift reception was the most critical moment of our fledgling relationship. This present represented how much she loved me and how well she knew me, the test of whether or not we were meant for each other.

And as I opened it, her hummingbird heart hung in space.

"What's this?" I asked.

Not the response she was looking for.

I quizzically examined the item, then tossed it to the floor without opening it and went over to kiss her.

She was not having any of it.

"Lia, what's the matter?" I asked.

In an instant, Lia was bursting with puddles and snot.

Oh boy, I thought.

She mumbled something through her palms.

Why the heck was she crying? Lia continued to sob while I considered.

Nothing was coming to mind. I knelt beside her and said, "Lia, I think I would understand you better if you took your hands away from your mouth."

She mumbled something again. I listened but could not understand her. I shuffled closer and examined her chest to make sure oxygen was getting in.

"Uh, are you okay?" I asked. "You're mumbling."

She pulled her hands from her contorted face and made a noise. It wasn't the hands; there was no muffling device. That was just how she sounded.

I figured I'd occupy myself until she started making sense. The best thing was to leave her alone. I looked around for something to do in the meantime and saw the gift I had tossed on the floor.

I took it in my hands and raised it to eye level. It looked as if it were a Halloween costume—a skeleton suit, to be precise. In the lower left corner a yellow starburst exclaimed that the bones glowed in the dark. Maybe her moaning was a hint, I thought.

"You want me to be a skeleton for Halloween?" I ventured.

Her wailing increased. Did that mean I was on the right track?

"You want to see what I look like with no skin?"

Nothing.

"You want me to study anatomy with you?"

She gave an upper-lip quiver.

I didn't know what was going on.

Gradually, she settled down. She placed her wet hands on her knees and took a few deep breaths.

How could we be having a pleasant meal and conversation one moment, and the next have her crying on the couch?

I decided to get to the bottom of this. "Okay, Lia, why don't you explain to me why you gave me this?"

She took a breath and finally started speaking in English: "Remember, about six months ago [sniff, sniff], I was in your office, and there was a sticky-note on your desk?"

"Uh, sure." There were always sticky-notes on my desk. I sticky-noted everything.

"Remember what it said?"

"Yeah," having no idea, "but why don't you tell me."

"It said 'flesh suit.'"

Flesh suit? Why would I have a sticky-note that said "flesh suit"?

"Well," she continued through her sniffles, "you told me that all you wanted in life was to have a flesh suit like Slim Goodbody on Saturday morning cartoons."

Oh, yeah. I *did* want one of those. Slim Goodbody was so cool. He wore a flesh suit—half bone, half muscle—and sang songs about eating fruits and veggies. I had been joking around with one of my co-workers about the suit and how I had wanted to know the names of all the bones and muscles. It would be easier to recall which leg bone was the femur and which one was the libya (or is that a country?) if I could just look down on my flesh suit and see. I could wear it to parties. I could point out to the guests where, in my small intestines, the cream puffs and stuffed mushrooms were lodged. It would be great.

"So for the last couple of months," Lia said, "I've looked everywhere for a flesh suit, and all I found was this skeleton outfit—and you hate it." She started to cry again.

"Lia, I understand now. This is perfect. This is much cooler than Slim's flesh suit. This one glows in the dark!"

I opened the package and pulled out the polyester and rubber. It looked like fabricated fossils from a *Jurassic Park* movie set.

I counted the ribs. "See, one, two, three. I didn't know the body had three ribs."

"There are twelve!" sobbed Lia.

"Well, now I know. If this suit wasn't wrong, I probably would have gotten mixed up and counted only eleven or something."

Lia didn't laugh.

"Tell you what." I started putting on the black fabric over my clothes. "Let's try this sucker on for size."

I put my legs through the slit down the skeleton's back and hung the fabric on my shoulders.

I looked ridiculous. The suit was enormous. It must have been made for a Neanderthal. My rubber arm bones were past my real hand bones. I was standing on my leg bones. I looked down at the package; in small letters in the bottom right corner it said "XXL." They were almost illegible. Obviously, Lia had not noticed them.

"Cool," I said, grinning. "These bones are so big!" I looked down at my pelvis, which was knocking between my knees. The image sent me laughing uncontrollably.

Lia couldn't keep from laughing either. I swung my radius and ulna over to her face so that she could wipe her tears. In seconds, we were bent double and belly-aching.

The hilarity was incurable. I hadn't laughed like this in a long time.

"Hey, I've got an idea," I said, and put my two legs into one leg of the bone suit. "Come on in." I took one arm out of its sleeve.

Lia got up and put her legs in, grabbed me around the waist, and slipped her arm up to the giant skeleton elbow.

She felt warm against my body. She was holding me tight, probably for balance, but I knew it was for love. We swayed back and forth in a two-dimensional skeleton dance.

"Let's turn off the lights," I suggested.

We hopped over to the light switch and examined our figure. We were one big, glowing cartilaginous framework. I kissed Lia. "Thanks for the flesh suit. It has really brought us closer together."

"Ha, ha," said Lia, unmoved.

Since then, Lia and I have gotten a lot better at both giving and receiving gifts, though we've had some close calls. There was the August blunder when I forgot Lia's birthday, the Christmas snafu when I gave Lia the camping equipment I wanted, and the Valentine's Day when I ruined our white carpet. But either out of love or the remembrance of the birthday when she gave me an anatomically incorrect, oversized skeleton suit, she has kept her mouth shut.

To alleviate the risk of giving the wrong thing, I have begun writing down exactly what I want. This year for Christmas, I asked for magnetic poetry, glow-in-the-dark ceiling stars, and three plain T-shirts of different colors. Of course, she could have figured that out all on her own, but why chance it?

Lia thinks the above strategy is a cop-out. She still wants me to guess what to get her. Sometimes I get it right, and when I do, it's like sitting in that parade convertible with the ticker tape raining down. Other times, my gifting produces results less exemplary. She feigns excitement and asks if I kept the receipt (which I have learned to do).

Trying as they are, gifts, I've learned, are good. Good to receive, good to give. My advice to those of you who, like Gary, are giving or receiving a gift anytime soon is to be gentle with one another. Wrapped in that smooth paper is more than a Hallmark card and a Halloween costume: there's a heart.

Chapter Nine

Valentine's Day Massacre

Three holy gentlemen have been credited as the true Saint Valentine.

One man, a priest named Valentine, lived during the third century under the rule of Claudius II. Claudius had this idea that single men made better soldiers than married ones (he must have known some wimpy married men like me), so he gave a decree that no member of the Roman army could marry. Valentine, the romantic that he was, believed this to be cruel and unusual. He therefore decided to perform secret marriage rites for military men in love. Claudius found out, Rome killed Valentine, and the rest was history.

Another story describes a Valentine who also had an inclination toward subversive action. He, too, lived in third-century Rome, but this time it was he who was in love. He loved God. And I guess that was illegal, so he was executed on, of all dates, February 14 in the year AD 269.

A third, more romantic story contends that Valentine was in prison and fell in love with a young woman who tended to him. The female, according to legend, happened to be the daughter of the jailer, and believe it or not, her father was not happy about the affair (even though the history books stress that the relationship was purely platonic). Allegedly, before getting the ax, Valentine sent a farewell letter to his girlfriend, signing it "from your Valentine."[5]

Some scholars believe that these stories should be credited to a singular Valentine, yet the Catholic Church recognizes all three as separate individuals. Some sects acknowledge others as the true Valentine. I suppose it doesn't really matter.

Regardless, each legend relates that there was a guy who loved love and died because of it.

For those of us who have spent a Valentine's Day or two drowning sorrows with our friend Jack Daniels or blowing bubbles in an ice cream float (which has always been my beverage for coping and moping), the connection seems appropriate—love and death, death and Valentine's Day, Valentine's Day and torture.

More often than not, February 14 falls on the wrong day, if you know what I mean. Love is way too fickle, way too inconsistent to celebrate on a particular day. I'm either not in a relationship or in a dying one—or, if I'm in one, the special day doesn't measure up to expectations and puts the relationship in jeopardy. Valentine's Day, as far as I can tell, is a lose-lose proposition.

Why do we torment ourselves? Why is love, or lack thereof, worth feeling this awful? And why do we tolerate the existence of a day that calls attention to how unloved we feel?

We deserve more, darn it. Life is hard enough without days to remind us of what we are missing. Maybe we were meant to remain lonely. Maybe Valentine's legacy is to warn us that if love is our goal, the price is pain and death. Yet, knowing the price, we still strive like Sisyphus, always hoping that one day we will surmount the summit of love and be whisked away into a world where it is February 14 every day, and each one of them is perfect. Hey, I would settle for just one.

We deserve one perfect Valentine's Day. Just one—one sweep-off-the-feet, soar-to-the-clouds-and-never–touch-down day of romance before we die. That's not too much to ask.

As for me, I'm still waiting. With the exception of Valentine's Day 2003, I've managed to ruin every one.

Valentine disappointment started early for me, even during those formative Februaries in elementary school when you had to give little prefab Snoopy, GI Joe, or Strawberry Shortcake cards to every classmate—even that girl who pulled your hair so hard you cried in front of all your friends, even that boy who punched you in the gut and knocked the wind out of you during recess and left you for dead, even your teacher who had a nose like a witch. Everyone. Mom never understood. She never saw the day for what it really was: a brilliant conspiracy, created by card-manufacturing lobbying groups, who were working in cahoots with the unified candy workers of the world to force schoolchildren to buy more valentines and sugary hearts than necessary, in order to boost their profits during the shortest month of the year.

Most of the valentines I received were innocuous, the more memorable from friends who had signed them Eileen Dover, Seymour Butts, or IP Daily. I usually signed mine "Ned."

But in Mrs. Franchesco's fourth-grade class, I decided to lay it on the line. For the first time in my short life, I decided to take the leap into the pit that is love.

I had fallen for an angel of a lass by the name of Stephanie Fitzpatrick. God, was she beautiful. She wore her hair in a ponytail and had a smile that could melt Antarctica. She was also a master kickball player and could out-sprint most of us guys with one leg tied behind her back. She had been in my third-grade class as well; I had been in love with her for more than a year. So as February 14 approached, I could not hold in my feelings any longer. I decided to conjure Cupid out of mythological hibernation and request him to loose an arrow for me.

I saved the most suggestive valentine for her, a red and pink card with Winnie the Pooh hugging a pot, which read "Bee my Honey." I cupped it in my shaking hand and admired the half-moons of Pooh's eyes. My heart raced as I signed the back, "To Steph … Love, Ned." I slipped the smooth card stock into the envelope sliver and prayed for a positive response.

Man, how the butterflies stirred! How the butterflies stir even now as I write! In four little words, written on a tiny piece of paper and slipped into a miniature envelope, I had managed to fit my entire heart—all that I felt for the love of my life.

The next day in Mrs. Franchesco's class, we walked around with our stacks of industrialized love-note propaganda and placed cards in boxes on each person's desk. I lingered too long before Stephanie's; realizing that my friends' eyes would be on me soon, I took a breath, prayed on the wings of Cupid that she would reply to my note with one of her own, and gently placed little Pooh in her box.

She never answered. Not ever. Stephanie Fitzpatrick never told me she loved me back, never shared what she thought of me, never mentioned whether she liked Pooh's pun. In her defense, I didn't ask her a question. Anyway, she probably received a hundred cards with "Love" scrawled next to a name. Stephanie was a goddess. Maybe saying nothing was the gentlest way of letting me down.

I eventually got over her. My crush only lasted six years—six years of sweaty palms and drippy armpits whenever she was within foul-shot range, six years of miniature heart attacks and swollen tongue-ties when she addressed me (which happened thrice), six years of missed lessons while I daydreamed about holding her hand and carrying her textbooks and being mixed-doubles tennis champions of the world.

I never wrote her another valentine.

I didn't try my hand at Valentine-style romance again until college, and the result was not much better. It nearly killed me.

My buddy Pasqual had the idea of baking cookies and crafting valentines for fifty of his friends and signing each one "Love, Barry and Levon" (from the MTV cult show *The State*). It was like being a secret admirer to everyone. All girls like secret admirers, Pasqual explained, and all he needed was to have one in fifty, or 2 percent, of his valentines work for him to score a chick. He sold me on his stratagem over lunch in Vail Commons; he said he was sure his plan would provide me a chick as well. He needed a Levon, not to mention someone to help bake the five hundred cookies, make the heart-shaped cards, and deliver them all before six the next morning. Guess I was the only one dumb enough to think it was a good move.

So we—I mean Barry and Levon—sprung to action. It truly was an all-night affair. We cooked, we glued, we glittered, we delivered—and then we collapsed on our dorm mattresses and dreamed of the love wave we would shortly be riding.

A wave that crashed soon after dawn. Can you believe it? These girls, these friends of ours, felt offended by our tactic. Somehow being named one of fifty caused them not to feel special. For some reason, girls (at least these) wanted to be singularly admired, to be uniquely chosen, to be the one and only of Barry and Levon. By mid-morning they were united and looking for a Bastille to storm, ready to wage their own Reign of Terror. From the safety of our locked, second-story room in Watts Hall, Pasqual and I watched in horror as they sharpened their guillotines on the quad.

Good thing most of the women were unfamiliar with *The State* and spent their tempers looking for two guys actually named Barry and Levon. Pasqual and I prayed that these vengeful women would actually find them and that we would remain anonymous.

Days later, when the cookies were all eaten and the truth finally came out, the tide of tempers had fortunately receded, and we only had to endure a few howls of laughter at our expense. The damage could have been worse. However, in the months that followed, neither Barry nor I had luck with love at Davidson College. We graduated single.

He took a job crunching numbers in Charlotte and met a sweet girl who liked the mountains. They now live in western Carolina, Pasqual crunching numbers and sending them back to Charlotte via the Internet in between baby Punjab's naptimes. He couldn't be happier.

I married a girl from Wake Forest University and thought my Valentine woes were over.

But they had only begun.

I proposed to Lia on February 9, 2000. I spent months planning the event, endured the self-imposed humiliation of talking to her parents, and managed to surprise her with the most romantic proposal in the history of proposals. My strategy was to construct an event such that there was no way in Hades she could say no. And for the first time in my life, my plan went accordingly. I blew her away, pulled it off without a single hitch. Lia cried, laughed, convulsed, and said yes all at the same time. If love truly was a wave, she was lost in the undertow. It was the greatest triumph of my life.

But it wasn't Valentine's Day.

So five days later, when Lia and I met at her house on Polo Road, like we did most days after her med school classes, I was caught off guard when she huffed into the kitchen after I asked her, with my hands in my pockets, what she was making for dinner. She acted as if I had said something rude.

She must have had a rough day, I figured. *Better give her space.* So I went into the living room and flipped channels while she fixed chicken quesadillas for me.

Sitting across from me at the table, Lia didn't seem to have much to say, but by the way she was murdering her tortilla, I could tell something was bothering her. But what? I had no idea. Dinner tasted fine to me.

Soon, Lia's eyebrows started to converge; her upper lip shuddered, and I knew I was in trouble.

"What?" I asked in a declarative tone.

"Do you know what day it is?"

I thought for a moment. "Thursday? Oh, did you want to watch *Friends* or something?"

"It's Valentine's Day!"

"So?" I said.

"Didn't you plan anything?"

"No, was I supposed to?" I asked.

She put her silverware down and gripped the dining room table. Taking a measured breath, she attempted civility. "Well, most guys do. Most guys take their fiancées out to dinner." Her voice steadily increased in volume. "Most guys give their fiancées flowers and chocolates. Most guys give their fiancées sweet, romantic cards. Most guys don't ask their fiancées to cook them dinner while they watch TV! Most guys don't treat their fiancées like maids!" Her face matched my hair color. She quivered with anger.

"Well, sorry. Tell you what, if you have some markers and construction paper, I'll make you an awesome Valentine's card."

Lia huffed. "All a girl wants is a little romance on Valentine's Day. That is not too much to ask."

I pondered. "Okay. And I'll wash the dishes."

She picked up her fork, pointy part down, considered stabbing me, thought better of it, dropped the fork, and huffed again.

I couldn't believe it. There was Lia, huffing, accusing me of not being romantic. Me! Had she forgotten what lengths I had taken just five days earlier? Had she not understood how much work I put into that proposal? Had she any idea how expensive that ring on her finger was? I was getting mad. I was close to huffing myself.

What I hadn't understood was that Lia had experienced just as many Valentine disappointments as me. Her only admirer had been a guy named Sven. He was a blondie from Sweden who liked to tuck his T-shirt into his shorts. However, in the realm of romance, he put most men to shame. He wrote Lia love letters and gave her paintings of the two of them building sandcastles together on the beach. Once, during show-and-tell, he brought in a ring pop, the one he was going to give Lia when he was old enough to ask her to marry him. He was five. On Valentine's Day, he baked Lia a cake and wrote *Jag a"lskar dig* ("I love you" in Swedish) in blue and yellow icing. Lia thanked him and ate it with her parents. Over the summer, he moved back to Sweden and lost Lia's mailing address. Lia never received a true Valentine again. She thought now that she had me, she would never suffer another February 14 misfortune.

She deserved more, darn it. She deserved love. She deserved one perfect Valentine's Day—just one. That was not too much to ask.

Somehow we got through it; we didn't even postpone the wedding. But the process taught me several important lessons: (1) love today does not guarantee love tomorrow; (2) when it comes to love, we always want more; and (3) I better do something next Valentine's Day—or else.

Before long, Valentine's Day 2001 was approaching like a deadline.

I knew I had to come up with something—something loving and memorable, something to make her feel special, something to keep her from huffing and picking up pointy forks. So on Valentine's Day morning I sat down at my desk and wrote out a list of all the romantic stuff I could think of: flowers, candles, fire, steak, streamers, etc. I took the afternoon off and set plans in motion.

And I have to admit, I did well.

Lia came home at dark. I met her at the door with an eyebrow raised and a collared shirt unbuttoned like Don Johnson. Behind me, red cinnamon-smelling candles marked a carefully spaced path across the carpet of our condo. The lights were out, save for the dancing glow from the candles' hooked wicks. Plucked rose petals laced the candles together, leading to a blanket on the living room floor before our hearth. In the fireplace crackled a Duraflame log to be mesmerized by.

She dropped her bag and leapt into my arms, hugging my neck and hooking her legs around my waist. Tenderly and deeply she kissed me while I carried her through the maze of fire to the picnic blanket. Flames reflected and sparked in her dark eyes.

I poured her some wine, this Shiraz stuff I knew she liked, and brought out shrimp cocktails that looked like a school of pink-bottomed mermaids diving into a sea of molten lava. We fed each other while she stared at me with that twinkle that triggers a reaction down below. We held off dessert until later. I went back to the kitchen and organized our main course: steak, which I had overcooked, and baked potatoes, which I had undercooked. Both were tough. We chewed, grimacing, until our jaws hurt. Yet the fire was still in her eyes. I knew I had not failed. We made love among our dishes and watched the Duraflame smoke and smolder.

We didn't notice the cinnamon-smelling coagulated catastrophe until it was too late. Red perfumed wax had melted, accumulated, and spilled all over our white carpet.

For all intents and purposes, the night was over. Lia briskly clothed herself, pulled her hair back, and refused to acknowledge my existence. Sighing, I embarked on a long, cold night of de-waxing. We pried the affixed candles from the floor fibers and exhausted our cleaning sprays, scrub brushes, hot rags, and wits.

When all was said and done, it looked like we had performed our very own Valentine's Day massacre at 2105 Aspen Way (an obscure Chicago suburb about 750 miles from Michigan Avenue). Capone would have been proud.

We didn't learn until later that the only way to eradicate candle stains is with brown paper bags and an iron.

Even the best-laid plans of mice and men ...

Was I destined, or rather doomed, to disaster? Maybe the price you do pay for love is death. Sorrowfully, I realized no such thing as a perfect Valentine's Day existed. Or so I thought until 2003, when I gave Lia hers.

Lia and I were doing better than ever; she would be finishing medical school in a few months, and we had recently sealed our fate and sent in our Residency Match List.

The process to decide where to do one's residency is a unique one. During the fall and winter of their final year of school, medical students apply to the programs they are interested in attending, and these programs choose a number of applicants to interview. From these interviews, the students and the programs rank each other. These "rank lists" or "match lists" are then sent into a centralized data center where a supercomputer performs some high-level mathematics and spits out the location where each medical student will spend his or her next three to seven years. Once this happens, there is no more choice in the matter. Wherever the computer tells you to go, that's where you go. Sometimes the matrix fails to match people, and students then have to participate in "The Scramble," a frantic, disorderly dash to fill all remaining program slots. This process is the closest thing I have ever experienced to having one's fate sealed. It was one of the biggest decisions of our lives, and we had little control over it. In a way, it was actually kind of freeing.

So the last several months had been filled with interviews and imaginations of future places and a new life together. Pediatric residency, to us, was a three-year opportunity to go anywhere. It was a chance of a lifetime.

I suppose some would consider residency a three-year prison sentence of fatigue and indentured labor. And in the crock pot of our emotions, mixed in with the herbs of hope were dashes of fear and pinches of worry. No doubt Lia was entering the toughest, most exhausting years of her life. My situation wasn't much sweeter. I was leaving a great job to travel to a city where I knew no one and had no job. We had our share of stress, yet we were excited. We would have each other, and for once that seemed like it would be enough.

Though we loved living in North Carolina and were given the choice to stay, we decided that we would try a different part of the country. After all, it would only be three years. We were like the dog Buck, head down and arms crossed by the campfire, hearing the wolves call his name. Lia and I were ready to try something new, to heed the call of the wild.

Early in our residency search, I had brought home a discarded corkboard map of the United States, thinking we could label potential cities with pins. We quickly narrowed our relocation search down to the ten coolest cities in America with good pediatric programs, and ranked and re-ranked them periodically as fall transitioned into winter. We were geographical acupuncturists. It felt like a game. It felt like *The Price is Right*. But whether we won the Showcase Showdown or not, the process made us richer and brought us closer together. Mailing in the Match List, however, made it all become very real, very fast. Something about a sealed fate really makes you cuddle more, like falling into love in a broken elevator.

Like I said, Lia and I were doing great, feeling great, and it was in that splendid state of serenity that the shroud over romance lifted. I received an epiphany—I thought of the greatest Valentine's surprise ever.

It was a hazy morning, still dark. Lia, as usual, had a full day at the hospital, so we had decided, with my secretive and subtle nudging, to meet downtown and eat breakfast together at a favorite little bakery I had frequently talked about but had never taken her to. We would need to drive separate cars, so I left her brushing her teeth and hair at home and told her to meet me at my office. I needed to pick up a couple of things on the way.

Lia is incredibly go-with-the-flow; she never has the least suspicion. She makes surprises too easy. *I should do these kinds of things more often*, I thought while waiting on my car hood for her to arrive.

Her yellow headlights gestured a greeting as they entered the empty lot, and I hopped off my hood to meet her.

Joining hands, we started walking up the numbered streets of downtown Winston-Salem (away from the bakery, but Lia didn't know, and toting a loaded backpack, which Lia hadn't noticed).

Everything in Winston-Salem ties together. First established as a Moravian settlement in the Wachovia Valley in 1753 by a group escaping religious persecution, it was then called Bethabara (the place of healing in the ford of the Jordan River). Eventually, the simple and saintly settlers were stable enough to develop a central city they named Salem. According to history, it was a happy little place, a content community at peace with itself and its neighbors—neighbors who, decades later, turned out to be a group of Quakers. The Quakers named their parcel of earth Winston, and, being a slightly more entrepreneurish bunch, began successfully manufacturing and selling commodities such as textiles and tobacco.

Within a few years the borders of Winston began to press in on the white fences of Salem. But instead of fighting, the towns decided to hyphenate. They—pardon the pun—smoked the proverbial peace pipe, and tobacco soon became the city's largest employer. By the late 1800s, Winston-Salem had become the wealthiest city in the state. Therefore, in order to secure their newfound prosperity, the bright people of the Wachovia Valley funded and filled two banks with their money.

Unfortunately (for the people of Winston-Salem), the Great Tobacco Settlement cut the mighty tobacco giant into a third of its former size. As a result, the economy took a downturn, one of the banks sold a building and moved the headquarters to Charlotte, and the tobacco company bought a food company and encouraged smokers to kick their habit by eating cookies. The effect seemed good; the number of smokers dropped drastically. However, the good people of the hyphenated city quickly moved on from the cookies and assuaged their nicotine cravings with "Hot Now" glazed doughnuts from a fledgling fried dough bakery that soon became a national phenomenon. In time, Forsyth County stabilized financially.

Sadly, however, because of the high rates of doughnut consumption—and no nicotine to curb the appetite—the obesity rate grew exponentially, drastically increasing the number of heart-disease and lung-cancer patients. This necessitated the presence of a hospital. Consequently, the largest business in Forsyth County is now a hospital—a place of healing and the home of Wake Forest University Medical School, where Lia was enrolled. Everything in Winston-Salem ties together. Maybe it's the hyphen.

To continue with the theme, I had close friends who leased the top floor of the vacant bank building, which was the location of my surprise.

I got chills as I walked with Lia down Third Street, thinking how reality makes such a great story. When we entered the lobby, Lia gave me a look that said, *This can't be Ollie's Bakery, can it?*

I signed us into the guest logbook and guided her to the elevator. My finger traced the numbers until I reached the top one. I pressed it, and we were propelled to the tallest point on the city's skyline.

Someone was waiting for us. She guided us through unlocked doors to the southeastern corner of the building. Lia gave me another look. I did my best not to smile too much. Taking the knob in hand, I opened the corner office door and let Lia walk in first.

The walls of the room were windows that stretched from ceiling to floor. A tablecloth and roses covered the rickety card table I had found in a supply closet. Twisted streamers garlanded the perimeter from the ceiling. Lia admired the decorations and walked to the window, curling her toes to the edge of glass. She pressed her nose to the pane and took in the pink hints of morning that were yawning on the horizon. I flicked a match to light two candles. And as Lia picked out landmarks along the skyline, I pressed play on the CD player hiding under the table.

I took her hand and turned her toward me, and we danced in the morning from our corner cubicle penthouse in the sky.

While we twirled, she read the banner I had erected the previous day:

Chez Erickson ... le Petit Dejeuner.
Le Menu: le pain, le fromage, le fruit, le café, et l'amore.
Bon appetit!

She rested her head in that hollow above my clavicle, and our dancing became swaying and then stillness. I asked her if she was ready for breakfast, helped her to her seat, and revealed one by one the contents of my bag—pastries and coffee from my favorite little bakery that she had thought we were going to that morning. We said grace, and as she opened her eyes, I held a card open for her to read. The words described a surprise weekend getaway I had planned. I sensed she was nearing love overload.

I twisted the top off the coffee and poured. "Un café, si vous plait?"

"Bien sur, mon cheri." Lia has a great accent.

"I'm not a cherry."

"No, you're not," she said, smiling.

We clinked cups ... and were blinded by the morning rays while we laughed coffee up our noses and held hands across the tablecloth, reminiscing about the life we had been given. We wished it would never end.

Lia squeezed my fingers and said, "This is the greatest Valentine's Day ever." And it was ...

Until I realized I was wrong: one perfect Valentine's Day isn't enough. And once you set the bar high, there is only one way to go. I sensed this as we closed in on another Valentine's Day. Lia wanted more. But we lived in Denver now, and I didn't know anybody who leased top floors of buildings.

Why do expectations increase? Why can't one perfect day of romance be enough? Del Amitri, one of my favorite songwriters, sings, "Life ain't worth living without a little love, but a little love is never enough."[5] He couldn't have sung or written it better. We all want more. We always want more. We are never loved enough.

Lia's never satisfied. I'm never satisfied. You're never satisfied. Our dog is never satisfied.

I have a theory about this. I may be way off, but here it is: each one of us has an infinite need for love. We will never receive enough love to quench the need inside. We will always hunger for more. Kind of depressing.

Ah! But here's a thought: we were made this way on purpose. God created us this way for a reason—not because He is mean, but because He has an infinite supply of love. Only a heart big enough to hold an infinite supply is big enough to receive an infinite supply. He wants us to receive all of His love. So He made our hearts big enough to fit Him—large enough to hold all of His love.

So the love I'm used to chasing after won't be enough, even if I catch it. It won't completely satisfy. It might satiate my appetite for a day, even a year—it might satisfy me like a Snickers—but sooner or later I'll be hungry again.

I am hungry all the time. I have a love-hunger comparable to the appetite of a Tyrannosaurus rex.

But I believe one day all this will change. One day, down this road called, for lack of a better word, Life, I'm going to sit down to a feast. This, by the way, is the description Jesus gives of heaven. And a voice will say, "Come. Eat. Be satisfied." And I will soak in the spread, which will contain all my favorite stuff. It's going to be love-food. And I'm going to pig out … forget the silverware. I'm going to eat like a Viking. And it's going to be perfect.

Until then, I'll suffer and starve through imperfect Valentine's Days, and poor Lia will suffer and starve through Valentine's Day disappointment. I guess we'll just hunger together until we enter that corner cubicle penthouse in the sky and eat the food of Life—eat until we're full, and never want again.

Chapter Ten
New Carpet

It wasn't the Valentine's Day Massacre that finally finished off our carpet; it was Ella the Retriever. We hid the candle stains by buying a little rug for our entryway and strategically rearranging our furniture. It wasn't rocket science, more like furniture Twister. After all was said and done, I thought the ruined carpet had a fighting chance of sticking around awhile—plus we had the added bonus of the cinnamon scent. Ella's contribution, however, delivered a final, knockout punch.

Some of our friends use a certain categorical system for the people in their lives, and Lia and I have adopted it, too. In essence, friends can be classified by the amount of time you can enjoy their company before the fun wears out. For instance, there are *evening-ers*—people you would gladly share dinner with, but not a whole day or weekend or week. Those would be *day-ers* or *weekend-ers* or *week-ers*, depending on how long you can bear each other. Correspondingly, you can have *afternoon-ers* or *hour-ers* or *barely-get-through-a-cup-of-coffee-ers*. Some friends are just better taken in tiny doses.

In no way are any of the categories bad; some of our best friends are afternoon-ers—we can go for a picnic, play some frisbee golf, and pick out shapes in the clouds until the cows come home. But once the cows come, it's best to part ways. They start looking at their timepieces; my pants start feeling uncomfortable; Lia starts stifling yawns. Sometimes it is best to cut bait. Because if you attempt extending an afternoon-er relationship into the evening, you could end up in trouble. You start talking politics or religion, and by the end of the night you are ready to kill yourself. You wonder, *Why am I friends with these people at all?* They wonder the same about you, and a fine friendship falls into jeopardy when all would have left happy if you had left it at just a picnic. Lia would have leaned to Eileen and said, "Let's do this again sometime." And Eileen would have said to Frank on the way home, "My, aren't the Ericksons nice?"

Of course, there are other people with whom you would gladly spend the whole day or entire weekend. For whatever reason, these friends are more tolerable over time. Again, they are not necessarily better friends; they are just easier to cohabit with. They like the same cereal and television shows; making decisions with them on a restaurant doesn't make your brain ache.

The categorization method works up and down the scale, from the nice checkout-line lady who is a *cordial-few-seconds-er*, all the way up to the precious few, those kindred spirits, those gifts from an Almighty who must love us, those whose parting does cause such sorrowful sweetness that you have played with the idea of pooling resources and buying a house together. These are the *lifers*, the ones with whom you plan to grow old, live on the same cul-de-sac, and move in as neighbors at the Twilight Acres Retirement Community.

Lia and I have been graced with a lot of friends. For that, we are eternally grateful. However, we only have a few lifers, two of whom are Cooper and Beth Williams.

And you know you have a lifer friendship when the relationship survives a monumental dog crapping.

Some friends had invited the Williamses to take a jalopy Winnebago trip across the country: visit some sights, gamble for three days in Vegas, and tour some national parks with the winnings or the money scraps, depending on casino luck. How could you say no to that? So they asked us if we could watch their puppy, Ella.

No problem; we loved Ella. Even Chelsea, our socially inept springer spaniel, loved her. Chelsea believed herself to be human, or at least wanted us to believe she was. Whenever another dog interacted with her, she got this quit-blowing-my-cover look. For some strange reason, she would rather sit at the feet of Homo-sapien company than play with the barkers in the backyard. But after several introductions, Chelsea got along with Ella, and Ella got along with everything. As far as we could see, things would be just fine.

So Cooper and Beth dropped Ella off as they headed out of town. We said goodbye and wished them lucky slots; they wished us happy pantings. We would miss them while they were gone. They left us with the famous last words of dog-sitting: "Our dog never goes to the bathroom in the house."

(We have used these words, too. And Chelsea never does, in our house. But all bets are off in someone else's. Incidentally, we dropped off Chelsea at a house a few months ago, and as I was uttering those very words, I looked over at my nearly perfect dog squatting amidst the dining room chairs.)

Ella is a sweet dog, and I doubt she has any memory of the events that transpired. And we harbor no ill feelings. I'll give her the benefit of the doubt—had the following days not abided by the inevitability of Murphy's Law, she probably would have kept her business to the woods behind our place.

It was August 9, 2001; I remember it was cloudy. August in North Carolina normally isn't, which is probably why I remember it—that, and it was the day my grandmother died.

She was the greatest woman I had ever known, married to the greatest man there ever was. My grandparents were my mentors, my role models, my heroes. My favorite place in the world was their ranch outside of Rolla, Missouri. My best childhood memories were of horses, flips from the rafters into hay, walks next to Grandpa's knee to the barn to check on the cows. My favorite games were from the stories that came out of my head and into the plastic cowboys and Indians they set up in my corner of the family room. My favorite meals were the long ones listening to Grandma tell stories about mom's and my aunts' childhood, and watching Grandpa nod off into his chin as the glow of dusk faded.

What I loved most was how my grandparents loved each other. When I was a kid, it might have been how they loved me, but as I grew, I began to recognize the beauty of their ripened romance—their dances to no audible music, their embraces that knew no timetable, the way they talked about each other like the other was a treasure. I loved being at the ranch; I loved even more being with them. I loved how Grandma would call, "Bernie!" if she needed more birdseed from the shed; I loved even more how Grandpa would say, "Yes, Mom," and walk in his moseying way out the door. I loved hearing their love story; I loved even more watching the light in their eyes as they looked at each other while they shared it.

I was in the living room when my mother called. I wasn't too sad; I had known it was coming. Even saints don't live forever.

I remember a story Grandma told me: *Once there was a beautiful Chinese vase. It had pictures of little children and dragon tails and little firework explosions. It was a very expensive vase, and one day it fell—shattered into a thousand pieces. I was very sad because it was very beautiful. But when everything broke, the inside was revealed: there was a candle, a burning candle. I wondered how the candle got inside and how it had survived the fall. I watched it, wondering if there was anything I should do, when a pair of hands appeared from outside the picture. I didn't see a body, just a pair of strong hands. One by one they put the pieces back together. The glass cut his fingers, but he kept working on the vase. I never saw his face, only his hands. And when the vase was complete, it was more beautiful than before because the light shone through the cracks. Oh, it was so beautiful.*

"There is beauty in the brokenness, Ned," she would say to me. Beauty in the brokenness. The year preceding my grandmother's death was a broken one, and it was hard to see anything beautiful in it. In many ways, Grandma died on February 26, 2000, the day Grandpa did. Her will to live broke into a thousand pieces, but the candle inside just wouldn't go out. It didn't get the message.

I remember her hair in the mornings, dripping like branches on a willow tree, silver in the cool light of dawn. She would brush it with long strokes as if she were strumming a harp. In a twist and an instant, her locks would disappear, hidden in a bun. She always kept them in a bun. But in those last years, she spared herself the hassle, letting her hair fall over her shoulders like a funeral shroud. She spent most of her days wearing a robe, unmotivated to change her clothes. She complained of pain—pain when she sat, pain when she walked, pain when she lay down, and pain when she stood up. She had pain everywhere, all the time. My parents and relatives tried new furniture, pads, and other things. But nothing made her comfortable. Nothing can comfort a broken heart.

It became apparent she could not live alone. She left the ranch, and her daughters rotated responsibility, taking her in over the next year and a half. It was very taxing and traumatic. She was numb and wanted to die, and my mother and her sisters grew concerned. Drugs could not quell her depression; therapy had no positive effect. She spent a few weeks in a psychiatric hospital before wasting away in a sterile, peaceful nursing home. She never saw the ranch again.

The funeral was in a couple days, in Cambridge, Ohio. We made work arrangements and asked our friend, Jason, to dog-sit.

Lia asked if we should try to contact Cooper and Beth, but they were in a Winnebago, midway through the Utah desert. What were we to do, leave a general message in every RV campground within twenty-five miles of the strip?

It wasn't a big deal, I told Lia; it was only a few days. And Jason was a responsible guy. There was nothing to worry about (more famous last words).

I don't blame Jason for what happened. It wasn't his fault. It could have happened to anyone. And the crap was monumental.

———————————————— ———

It was cloudy on the day of the funeral. We had driven the five-hour span between Carolina and Cambridge the night before, and were back in the car by evening. Lia bought me some Buckeyes to cheer me, my first—I had always resisted because I thought they were nuts (which they are—poisonous ones—but they're also a type of candy made in the shape of the nut). We held hands for most of the journey home. Sweetness in the atmosphere.

It had been a long couple of days, with a lot of driving. I was happy to see our condo when its wooden exterior came into view. I pulled the key out from the ignition and grabbed our suitcase and garment bag; Lia unlocked the door.

We walked inside, and it smelled like poo. It looked like the smeared interior walls of a latrine. Chelsea greeted us at the door as if she had been through a bunker war. Ella pawed the sliding porch doors and left prints. There was a note on our kitchen counter from our dog-sitter that read "call me." We did, and he told us the story.

Ella had purportedly gotten into some discarded chicken scraps in the woods; our friend had found her gnawing on a drumstick in the middle of our living room. I assume she brought it in as a souvenir.

Before long she was in a corner taking care of business. And as Jason scurried to clean up the mess, Ella was in another corner unloading another log. Jason hurried over, and Ella wagged her tail into a bedroom and let loose on a chair. Yes, she crapped on the couches. She dropped bombs on the coffee table. She shot shrapnel on the wall. In a way it was rather impressive.

We surveyed the damage. There were feces everywhere: on the television, in the bathtub, on the Venetian blinds—*everywhere*. And this had been going on nonstop since three o'clock the day before. Jason claimed cleaning upward of fifty land mines before giving up. Why he hadn't simply moved her to the porch after the first log, I do not know. I cursed not owning a fence.

Tiptoeing through turds to the porch light, I saw Ella happy as could be, wagging and dancing in a layer of her own poo.

Lia erupted in tears. "Let's move," she said. "I can't live here."

"Lia, it's not that bad." I took a whiff. "Okay, it is."

We found room between brown smears on our love seat, held each other, and cried.

As we sat, another memory of my grandparents came to mind, another story Grandma used to share ... It was 1970. Grandpa and Grandma hadn't lived on the ranch very long. Grandpa had left his engineering job to teach at a local university, become a cowboy, and spend more time with his wife and girls. As smart a man as he was, he was pretty poor at business and had foolishly signed an extremely short mortgage with an outlandish payment schedule, which he soon realized he wouldn't be able to pay. He tried to refinance, but the bank wouldn't reconsider. They gave him two options: come up with the cash or lose the ranch.

One day he came home, and Grandma said he looked dead. His arms hung like a hanged man; his body slumped like a bag of flour. The bankers had told him they were going to foreclose. He walked into the house and met Grandma at the piano bench. They fell to the floor and into each other's arms. They cried and cried, and when the tears ran out, they kept crying on without them.

And somewhere in the sorrow, Grandma said God spoke ... She described it as a deep, slow voice. When she would tell the story and get to the part where God talked, she would swallow her chin into her neck and get real solemn: "God said, 'Remember this moment. It is the most beautiful moment of your life.' In fact, God said it twice," Grandma said, "just so I'd get it."

She loved to tell that story. Then, she would tell the one about the miracle of how they managed to keep the ranch. But I think she loved the first one more because they were the broken pieces, and in them a light was shining ... and over time, a pair of hands put them back together.

When I look back and think of my grandparents, that must be where the beauty came from—the light within; the light shining through the broken places of their marriage, of their lives; the light revealing the fact that they were only held together by grace, by love, by a pair of bloody hands ...

Lia and I cried and cried, and when the tears ran out, we kept crying on without them. We held each other amidst the mess. And in that moment I saw things with my grandparents' eyes: *This is the most beautiful moment of our lives. This is the most beautiful moment of our lives.* Two times, just so I'd get it.

I knew Lia wasn't ready at the time to share in my epiphany. For once, I kept my mouth shut, but it didn't change the holiness of the moment. It didn't matter how much crap was in the room. It was a beautiful aroma. Licking the tears off my upper lip, I smiled. In my mind I saw a picture: a beautiful broken vase, a beautiful broken boy and girl, holding one another, held together by a pair of hands.

We decided it was time to buy new carpet.

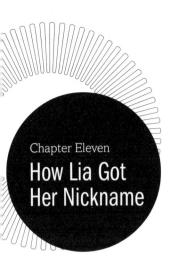

Chapter Eleven

How Lia Got Her Nickname

Ever since eighth grade and the pages of *One Flew Over the Cuckoo's Nest*, I've had a clear picture of what a psychiatric ward looks like. I suppose books, at times, exaggerate for effect or for lack of tamer words. Nonetheless, no matter how fictitious, books often lend themselves to believability, and I believed Ken Kesey's description of the halls and walls; the dirty, disheveled, sex-crazed wackos who lived within; and the evil beings like Big Nurse Ratched who watched over them. By the end of *Cuckoo's*, I vowed never to enter one of those places—especially as a patient.

So when my folks told me that Grandma was in a psychiatric hospital, that they were giving her electroshock therapy, all I could think of was McMurphy in the "Shock Shop." My sinews tensed; my neck muscles tightened. Some big nurse was torturing my hero.

I asked if she was okay. They told me to go and visit. I told them I couldn't: I had made a self-commitment.

Lia reassured me that my conceptions were amiss. The wards were, in her words, usually very quiet, very stable. She called it "structured serenity." The orderlies were generally very kind and caring. It was the "usually's" and the "generally's" Lia kept slipping in that reconfirmed my previous notions. I told her I didn't want to go. Maybe it was better to have my last memory of Grandma be a happy one. But even as I said these things, I knew I wanted to see her. Any encounter was better than no encounter, and opportunities were becoming few. I needed to take this one. And I loved Grandma.

And Grandma loved me. I had little doubt I was her favorite. When I came to visit, she always made my favorite desserts. She would take me to church, and people I'd never seen before would approach me and say, "You must be Ned. We've heard so much about you." I'd be helping with the dishes, and Grandma would seize me by the shoulders, turn me toward her gray eyes, and say, "I love you, my grandson. You are the most precious young man in the world." She had a way of making everyone feel like they were the most precious being in the world. She genuinely believed in the goodness of man and the ability of love to conquer all. And maybe she was right. There never was a single person who met Lena Sarchet who didn't love her or doubted that she loved them back.

Grandma never lived with Lia and me during that last year and a half of her life, which is probably why I minded her melancholy less than the rest of my family. I'm sure she was hard to live with. And I'm sure I had, even in the healthy years, an embellished impression of her. She wasn't perfect—she could be as ugly as anyone. As an outsider to her final months, I had thicker patience. Her perpetual complaining, persistent lamenting, and suicidal musing did not affect me or my thoughts toward her. She was in an incurable place. What she wanted she couldn't have, this side of heaven.

I waffled for days about whether to visit her, but finally made up my mind, and the next night Lia escorted my nervous legs toward the Crazy People Hospital where my poor Grandma was living. I was first struck by the number of plants and windows. A nurse sat on a couch with a remote control beside her. Like a child at the zoo,

I pointed at the woman as if she were an exhibit item; Lia blocked my arm. She told me later that the "nurse" was actually a patient.

"But she looked so normal," I replied.

"A lot of patients look normal," Lia explained. "Most patients stay only a few days."

We turned a corner and saw Grandma in her room. Her back toward us, she was reading old notes she had taken from ancient devotion times. Her bottom lip pooched; her eyes were searching for something on the page or something she had lost inside.

She did not notice our arrival. Lia waited in the frame of the door while I approached Grandma. I walked around the hospital bed and waited for her to realize I was there.

She didn't see me until I caressed her shoulder. The touch took her by surprise but strangely did not frighten her. As she turned, her countenance rose like morning sunshine.

"Oh, Ned!" She hugged me. She opened her eyes and saw Lia. Letting go of my neck, she reached out for my wife: "And Leela!"

Leela! Did Grandma just say *Leela*?

"Leela," Grandma said again, "it is so good to see you. Please, sit down." She grabbed the remote for the bed and adjusted the angled mattress flat.

I looked at Lia and with my eyes asked if she wanted me to correct Grandma.

Lia smiled and indicated no.

We listened while Grandma showed us around her room with her finger. She pointed to the cards she had received, then took her brittle Bible and pointed to the last few verses of Psalm 27, the passage she had been reading. She shared how difficult it had been to believe she might again feel and see the goodness of the Lord, but that the Lord wanted us to wait and be courageous. "Sometimes," she said, "courage for me is getting out of bed." She asked Leela how med school was going. Lia told her that she was tired but was learning all the time. "Be strong, Leela. Let your heart take courage—you will be the greatest pediatrician someday."

Lia blushed, feeling like the most precious girl in the world.

We spent close to an hour with Grandma, who never got Lia's name right. Lia didn't mind.

This was not the first time Lia and Grandma had spent time together. Grandma had even attended our wedding and written Lia notes. But to Grandma that night, and to me forever afterward, Lia was "Leela."

I hugged Grandma goodbye and felt her hand caress my hair. When we released, she took my hand in hers and placed it in Lia's, our three hands together like a team coming out of time-out. Grandma beamed and said, "You two are going to make it. You are going to have something special. A marriage for the ages. I wish Grandpa could be here to see it."

I was near speechless but managed to mutter, "I do, too."

"We love you," said Lia.

"I love you, Leela. We are honored to have you in the family," replied Grandma.

Walking away from the hospital, I squeezed my bride's hand and said, "Leela—I like the sound of that. What do you think?"

"It's okay," she said.

Leela. What a great nickname. Sweet, subtle, sincere. I've used it ever since.

Grandma went back to calling her "Lia." I don't know if someone corrected her or if that had simply been a one-night phenomenon. Nevertheless, her mistake was my gain.

Lia was silent about her feelings on being called "Leela." My suspicion was (and still is) that she liked the name. Even when I slip up in public, she rarely admonishes me. Like she did with Grandma that night, Leela has handled it—and me—with grace.

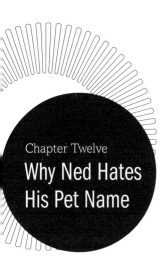

Nicknames are cool. My best friend growing up was bestowed the name "Cookie" by our soccer coach because he was always eating snacks during practice. Over the years, his title morphed, but the roots have remained. He now goes by "Cookiehead Jenkins," though his friends call him "Cook." Even in our thirties, I still call him by this moniker.

My big brother in our fraternity earned the nickname "Running Bare" for reasons not worth mentioning, but sadly the name that stuck was "Blimpo," for reasons not needing explanation. Fortunately for Bruce, college was only four years, and his nickname didn't follow him (though his large frame did).

Some famous people have endured, even exploited, their unusual physical characteristics—for instance, Carrot Top, Blackbeard, and Too Tall Jones. Other people have acquired nicknames for accomplishments on the field. Walter Payton was "Sweetness," Karl Malone was "The Mailman," and Joe Greene was "Mean." I don't know if Randy Johnson, "The Big Unit," got his name for physical prowess or athletic achievement. Either way, what a great name!

Nicknames are cool. I have always wanted one, but alas, it has not been my lot. It's like I wear a permanent nickname slicker that repels any label that might splash my direction. I've had some short-lived ones, usually mutated manipulations of my name: Nedski, Nedder, Nerd, Redhead Ned, etc. But nothing has stuck. My folks gave me such a unique name that no invention of man has been able to match or exceed it.

But there are other kinds of names ...

When you fall in love, you get another type of name. A pet name. Whereas nicknames have failed to stick, my sorry pet name is coated with super glue. I've done everything possible to get rid of it, but like a bad rash, it keeps coming back.

I gave Lia her pet name during Halloween. It was our first true holiday as a married couple, minus Yom Kippur, which we don't celebrate; Labor Day, which I don't know how to celebrate; and Columbus Day, which is not politically correct to celebrate.

As October 31 neared, we got more and more excited. I started wearing the skeleton suit. Lia went to Target and bought cardboard cats with green eyes and witches with flying brooms to put in the windows. We purchased a pumpkin from a church and carved the heck out of it. We named her (the pumpkin) Jackie and kept her until she rotted out and grew flies.

A few days before Halloween, we went to the grocery store for trick-or-treating supplies. We acquired enough candy to keep the Donner party alive through winter. On the way to my friend Rhoda, the cordial-few-seconds-er checkout-line lady, I spied a bin of mini pumpkins out of the corner of my eye.

Moved in the Halloween spirit, I turned to Lia. "Jackie needs some children," I said while tossing a couple in my cart.

Caught up in the moment, Lia grabbed another. "You can never have enough little mini pumpkins," she said.

I swiped my card and told Rhoda I would see her soon.

We wheeled to the car with bounces in our steps.

"Lia, I hope a ton of kids come to our house for Halloween, even though it would mean less candy for me."

"That is very generous of you," said Lia.

"I know. Can you believe it?"

Lia didn't answer, probably because she couldn't.

I tossed our newly purchased stash in the back seat. As we pulled out of the parking lot, Lia pulled out a mini pumpkin from the plastic bag. "Look how cute it is," she said as she stroked the orange skin with her finger.

"You're my little mini pumpkin," I said.

She batted her eyes.

"You can never have enough little mini pumpkin," I continued.

Lia is still my little mini pumpkin, though I only use the name on special occasions.

On the other hand, my pet name arrived with no story attached. It has no rhyme or reason. And Lia knows I hate it.

Ruthlessly, she uses it anyway.

Ugh. Should I say it? This is worse than the permission-from-dad story! This is another moment where skipping to the next chapter is permissible, maybe even advisable, and most certainly requested. Oh, well ... in the name of honesty ...

She calls me "Sweet Baby."

I hate it. I tell her so. I tell her every day.

It only gives her impetus to utilize it more.

A typical nightly conversation goes something like this:

As I'm reading in bed, Lia crawls up the covers like a lion.

"Hey, Sweet Baby," she says.

I shut the book. "You made me lose my place," I reply. "And, by the way, I am not a sweet baby."

"Yes, you are. You're my Sweet Baby."

"I'm not sweet, and I'm not a baby! Call me something else."

"Like what?"

"Something manly, like Hunky Man, or something."

"Okay, Hunky Baby."

"Hunky *Man*! I'm not a baby!"

"Sorry, Sweet Hunky Man."

"Hey, Leela, cut it with the 'sweet' stuff."

She'll then pooch her bottom lip and pretend to be upset.

"Leela," I try to explain, "I'm just worried that someday you'll accidentally call me 'Sweet Baby' in public. That would be humiliating."

"You don't want people to know you're my Sweet Baby?" she pouts.

"I'm *not* your Sweet Baby."

"Then whose Sweet Baby are you?" she asks.

"I'm nobody's Sweet Baby because I'm not sweet and I'm not a baby! I thought we covered this."

"Okay, Sweet Hunky Baby Man."

It's infuriating. It drives me insane. And someday, I swear, she'll push me over the edge, and I will go crazy …

But I won't mind. I won't fight one bit when the white-coat boys wrap me in straps and take me to the hospital. I will be just fine because I've learned that psychiatric hospitals aren't like the one described in *One Flew Over the Cuckoo's Nest*. They are sanctuaries of structured serenity. And if Lia comes to visit some evening and starts with that Sweet Baby crud, I'll just push the panic button and have a big nurse haul her away.

How's *that* for sweet?

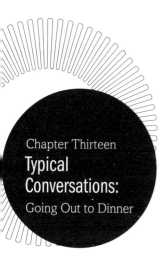

"Hey, Leela, where do you want to eat tonight?"

"I don't care. You decide."

"I don't care, either."

"Well then, just pick a place."

"Okay. Let's go to Brother's Barbecue."

"Nah," says Lia.

"How about El Taco?" I propose.

"Nah, I'm not in the mood for Mexican."

"We could go to Pasquini's Pizzeria."

"I don't really want Italian tonight."

"Leela, I thought you didn't care."

"I don't, but you haven't said Swing Thai yet."

"If you wanted to go to Swing Thai, why didn't you just say so?"
I ask.

Lia says, "Because I want you to want the same thing I want."

I huff. "So basically, you want a mind reader for a husband."

"No, I just want a husband who knows me."

"All right, next time you tell me to pick, I'll choose Swing Thai."

"But next time I might not want to go there."

"So how am I supposed to know where you want to go?" I ask, exasperated.

"You're just supposed to know. If you take the time to make sure we are on the same page, you will just know."

I almost quip, "So what you're saying is, the same page really means *your* page?"

But I'm hungry.

So instead I say, "Well, I actually wanted to go to Swing Thai in the first place. I was simply testing to make sure that I was right. Turns out, I was. Isn't that crazy? We both wanted to eat Taiwanese food."

"Liar," she says. "And by the way, Thai food is from Thailand."

"Let's just eat," I say, fooled again.

She smiles.

Leela grabs her purse, I grab the keys, and we drive two miles north to good old Swing Thai. And it doesn't bother me at all that we're not going to Brother's Barbecue or El Taco or Pasquini's, because between Leela and me, I was the one who really didn't care where we ate.

If all the mothers and young lasses of the world were simultane-ously zapped from earth and we men were left to our own devices, I'd say that 99 percent of us would eventually look like Jack from *Lord of the Flies*—and probably act like him, too. For whatever reason, boys prefer the natural state of things and the dirt that goes with it. Like most boys, I was a sporadic washer growing up. But all that changed in the fifth grade.

I really looked up to Robbie. He had brown hair and wore rugby shirts and used hair spray. The thing I admired about Robbie was his maturity. He was an expert in coolocity, having been introduced to all kinds of grown-up things before the rest of us because his sister was in high school. And because I was his friend, he would explain them to me. And because I wanted him to be my friend, I would pretend I already knew.

One morning before class, I walked up to a group of a half dozen gaping boys. Robbie was in the middle, telling them all that he took a shower every day before school. The way he described bathing made it sound both necessary and awesome. As I joined in the listening, I gaped alongside the others. I had never heard of such a thing.

Robbie put his hands in his pockets and rocked on his heels. "I can't even open my eyes until I take my morning shower."

The circle of us boys stood there, wondering if this could be true. Do cool people really shower every morning?

Robbie sounded so knowledgeable, so mature, so sure.

I noticed Stephanie Fitzpatrick listening in; she seemed so impressed.

I opened my mouth and lied, "Yeah, I've been showering in the morning so long I can't remember. It's the only way I make it to school awake."

Not so discreetly, I touched the left side of my hair in a vain attempt to conceal my obvious bed head. I doubt anyone believed me.

Robbie was kind enough to change the subject, proclaiming he stayed up every weekend to watch a show called *Saturday Night Live*.

I nodded along to his descriptions as if I knew what he was talking about, praying he wouldn't ask me a direct question about Mr. Bill—the guy seemed indestructible; he almost didn't sound real.

The next morning, to my mother's astonishment, I began a bathing ritual I have continued ever since.

It strikes me to think of how many showers that is: at least one a day for going on twenty years. And never once did it ever occur to me that there was another way, that Robbie had it wrong.

Lia had been selected to the pediatric residency program in Denver. It was a smooth but tearful transition for us. The moment Lia, Chelsea, and I mounted the U-Haul and shifted it into gear, we felt tremendous grief. It was like reaching the last page of a great book and having nothing more to read. I would miss my job—the challenge of keeping a nonprofit afloat, all the relationships with adults and kids, and the feeling that I was making a difference. Lia wouldn't miss medical school, but she was also sad to leave, for it marked the end of a significant chapter: eight life-changing years at Wake Forest University. Chelsea would miss the trees, the neighbor's cat she was never quite able to catch, and the oxygen. Most of all, we would miss our friends. Over the years, we had accumulated nearly too many (if there is such a thing): every type of friend from afternoon-ers to lifers. We were leaving them to move to a town 1,500 miles away, a place where we knew no one. We were also closing in on three years of marriage.

Lia's residency started in June 2003. I was fortunate enough to find a teaching job before we moved, and I was very excited about not having to start work until August. I had two months to do nothing but begin two of my lifelong quests: write the next Great American Novel and climb all the fourteen-thousand-foot peaks in Colorado (there are fifty-four in all, by most standards). Three years later, I'm still working on both. I'm further along on the mountains.

For some mountains, I would have to wake up early, sometime between three and four in the morning, in order to be able to ascend and descend before the daily afternoon thunderstorms. For other summits, I would leave for days, camp at the trailheads, climb at dawn, drive to the next mountain, fish in the evening, go to sleep at dusk, and do it all again the next day. It was this latter strategy I was utilizing while working down the Sawatch Range.

The Sawatch Range runs down the center of Colorado. The peaks are, in general, quite accessible for amateurs like me and include some of the most popular mountains in the state, such as the Collegiate Peaks (Mount Princeton, Mount Yale, Mount Harvard, and Mount Columbia) and the highest peaks in Colorado (Mount Massive and Mount Elbert, which are separated by twelve feet of elevation. You would think Mount Massive would be taller, but it's not).

That morning I had "bagged," as climbers would say, Mount Missouri before getting stormed off Elk Ridge on my way over to

Mount Belford and Mount Oxford. But even without these last two mountains, it had been a successful trip—five peaks in five days—and the effort had left its mark on my body.

I smelled.

Five days of sweat, dirt, woody campfire, and fish guts, sunbaked and all mixed together—the scent was profound and pungent. Driving home, the stench was almost overwhelming—so potent I kept sniffing under my arms in astonishment at the fragrance and retracting every time with a squinched-up nose and an "Oh!"

The thing was, after the thirtieth or fortieth whiff, I began to kind of like it. Each inhalation sent me into a higher state of incredulous ecstasy. It was like a drug. I smelled myself all the way home. I don't know, maybe it was the fact that once you hit fourteen thousand feet you start losing brain cells, but by the time my car and I spit out Turkey Creek Canyon into the Denver metro area, I was convinced that my body odor was heavenly, possibly marketable—if I could figure out how to bottle it.

It was me.

It was a "me potpourri."

I decided to name it "Man Smell." It was earthy, natural, primeval, rustic, rugged, manly, wild—words I liked, words I wished characterized me. And it was amazing; after only five days its smell was mine. I was fierce and strong. At least I smelled that way. I was a man, like Tim "The Toolman" Taylor. To smell my armpits after a long day's labor—why, it was like winning first and second prize.

As I drove, I lifted my right elbow and tilted my nostril low, and with sanguine joy I breathed in my salty, barky odor. I swayed backward in triumph. I thought of Walt Whitman's *Leaves of Grass*, rolled down the windows, and sounded my barbaric yawp over the roofs of the world: "I am man; smell my pits!" I was not a bit tamed.

I was in euphoria. I had entered enlightenment. I had discovered the best smell.

As I turned north on Santa Fe Boulevard, I thought, *Years ago, when my nose was attached to a child, I never had a problem with how I smelled. If I remember correctly, I liked all kinds of smells. I don't recall worrying about my breath. I was happy and content with a smell all my own. So what happened? Hmmm. Mothers. Mothers and their bathing fixations.* Through a dozen bottles of Johnson & Johnson No Tears Shampoo, I had received the unspoken message that my natural scent was something to be hidden. That to be a successful member of society (which for me meant attending preschool), one needed to smell like Rosemary and Jasmine (whoever they are).

I felt my face getting red and the fibers of the hair on my neck rising in anger.

What is wrong with the way we smell? Why do we in America choose flowers over le fumet au natural? *How much money—hundreds? Thousands?—do we spend each year on products to cover, conceal, and convert our man-smelling bodies into walking, talking torsos of fruit? What's with the trans-olfactorization? I bet if we all decided to boycott body-altering products, in a few weeks we would all be better off.*

I worked on a plan to bring about universal nose liberation. We, the people of the world, would go back to our olfactory roots. *I will preach of smelly bliss until the world wakes from its nostril hibernation. I will free the world from aroma addiction. We will learn to appreciate the distinct odors of each culture. We will realize that there is not as much separating us as we previously thought. We will become one. We will be free, liberated from the dominion of fragrance fascism.*

I stuck my head out the window and yawped. I shouted to the cars cruising alongside me, "Wake up! Wake up and smell yourselves!"

I wondered if Woman Smell was as good as Man Smell. Real Woman Smell. Not Victoria Secret, Chanel, Revlon, or some other smell, but pure, unadulterated, non-tampered female stench. Is that the stuff of dreams? I wondered how difficult it would be to convince Lia to try nose nirvana. She could be the first of my converts.

I daydreamed of a feral state the rest of the way home. By the time I reached civilization, I was convinced that showers were the root of all evil and that the true path to world peace began in putting down our bars of soap and loving each other just the way we smelled.

One thing was sure: I wasn't showering when I got home. I would wait with the flies circling my head for Lia to arrive from work. I would waft unadulterated pheromones throughout the house, and when Leela smelled me, she wouldn't be able to contain herself. She would rip her clothes off and then mine and carry me to bed, where we would make the wildest love of all time. She would floose up her hair and declare no showers for eternity. We would become jungle man and jungle lady and grunt to communicate and eat food without silverware.

Lia pulled into the driveway at a quarter to six that evening. I met her at the door with a smile and the rest of me.

Lia dropped her bags and her jaw.

"Ned, you smell," she said with a crinkle to her nose.

"I know, isn't it great?" I said eagerly.

"'Great' is not the word I'd choose."

"Captivating?" I tried.

"'Rank' is closer to what I was thinking," she replied.

"Good rank? Or bad rank?" I asked.

She gave me a look that said, *Do I even need to respond?*

"You mean you don't like my Man Smell?"

"Is that what you call it?"

"Man Smell. This is what Ned smells like. This is who I am. This is who you married." I revolved my torso and batted my stinky eyelashes. "Don't I turn you on?"

"You're turning my stomach," answered Lia.

"Aw, come here," I said. I reached toward her like Frankenstein.

"Ned, if you touch me, I will hurt you," she said with a serious look in her eye.

"Are you for real? You're asking me to give this up?" I said, pointing at my shirt.

"Only if you want this," as she pointed to her own.

I huffed.

We moved in from the door, and she started straightening the mess I had already made. I followed her around like a dog, wounded but still longing for affection.

Maybe she doesn't understand, I thought. *Maybe I need to explain what I found up in the mountains.*

As Leela walked resolutely around the house, I lectured to the back of her head all I had learned in the woods.

It didn't work. She took her coffee mug from her bag and began washing it.

I didn't like being ignored.

Slightly perturbed, I said, "So what you are saying is that your love is conditional. That you will only love me if I smell like flowers, like some tame, domesticated wuss of a male. Well, I'm sorry, but you married a real man, honey. This is what man smells like, and you are just going to have to get used to it, 'cause I'm a man, and it's about time I smelled that way. You're lucky you met me when you did, because if I smelled this way back then, girls would have been going crazy over me. It's fortunate you met me before I discovered Man Smell."

Lia kept tidying as if she were avoiding me. She was picking up clothes like she was weeding a garden.

I continued to press. "Leela, I know that Little Miss Priss voice inside of you is telling you to resist my irresistibility, but both you and I know that there is another voice, a truer, more primitive one, telling you that you must have me—you must have me now. It is urging you to tear your clothes off and make savage, wild love to me right now, isn't it? Don't deny it. I know it's there. It wants me."

Lia stopped and threw the armful of clothes she was carrying to the ground. She turned. There was fire in her eyes.

I misread them, thinking foolishly that my speech had worked. Any second now, she was going to rip those clothes off her body and have me for dinner.

I positioned my legs shoulder-width apart and steadied as she readied to pounce. I reached out my hands and pulled my fingers in unison back toward me. "I'm ready. Bring it on."

She breathed through her nostrils like a bull about to charge. Her eyes turned red. She was going to attack.

I gulped. She looked like more woman than I could handle. I shifted from leg to leg.

"You are too much," she said.

"Good too much? Or bad too much?" I asked, knowing the answer.

She gathered the clothes she had dropped and continued to the hamper. I followed dumbly. She walked over to the bed and sat Indian-style on it. Was she finally falling under my smell spell?

I walked quickly toward her. Abruptly, she motioned with her hand for me to stop.

"Ned," she said, her eyes turning gray as if a cold front had come in, "I was prepared to love you tonight."

"What do you mean, *was*?" I asked.

"I mean before you showed up looking like a Neanderthal and treating me like a cave-tramp," she answered. "You are not sleeping in my bed until you clean yourself up."

"You mean you are asking me to sacrifice my Man Smell?" I said weakly.

"Only if you want to be with me. I'm sure Chelsea won't mind sharing her mat with you. Of course, she might not want to sleep with you either."

"But …"

"Butt. That's right. You smell like butt. Now go take a shower before you permanently stain this place."

She got off the bed and walked briskly by; I breathed in the lingering scent of her perfume.

"Dang it," I said.

I turned on the faucet and stepped into the spray. Oh, the battles we choose to fight. Hanging my head, I watched brown dirt run rivulets down my legs. I was naked. I imagined I was a mighty Indian warrior fatigued from fighting, a hundred-foot waterfall pelting my skin with the pulse of the River Life. I shook my tresses back and forth and snorted as water went up my nose. Brown flecks of mud and rock stuck to the shower curtain. I guffawed. Man Smell fell from me, down a drain back to its origin.

I had bought this stuff called Tangerine Tickle a couple of weeks ago because I had finally run out of the free hotel shampoos I had compiled over the years. It smelled like what they want you to think Florida smells like—tangerines. I bought it because it was the cheapest. It doesn't tickle. I think they just included the word for the alliteration. I can appreciate that. I dabbed some in my right palm and lathered it in well.

Ned, Lia had said, *I was prepared to love you tonight.*

What a great line.

I smiled as I used my chest hair as a loofah.

She may have a sanitized Ned tonight, but Man Smell will be mine again tomorrow. She may have taken the wild smell out of the man, but she can't take the wild man out of me.

I tossed my mane. Water pulsated upon my face. I shut my eyes, opened my mouth, and sounded my barbaric-est of yawps over the rooftops of the world.

Falling into Love

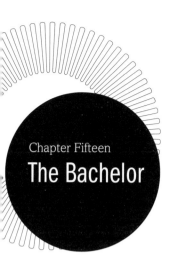

Chapter Fifteen
The Bachelor

Lia loves *The Bachelor*, the ABC "reality" show. She plans her week around it. Her devotion baffles—and haunts—me. I mean, why does she have to watch some show about love, starring some studly man, when she has me?

Once, I asked her why she loved it so—why Leela, the most brilliant and engaging woman in the world, a wife living blissfully in the united state of marriage, would attach herself to a television series with a predictable plot, dialogue punctuated by long make-out scenes, and fairy-tale romances that never worked out. I had painfully sat through an episode or two. All I saw was a glorified dating parade. Frankly, I couldn't decide what was sadder: the girls in the limo after they were dumped, confessing their pain and disappointment to a cameraman; or the very fact that they felt so hurt. After all, the guy they had "dated" had been "dating" a dozen-odd women at the same time. How hurt could you really feel?

Lia said she loved it because the show is about love. "How could you not love a love story?"

"Well, Leela, for 95 percent of the participants, the show is about rejection."

"No, it's not. It's about who gets the final rose and the journey it takes to get there and the hope that love has given two people. The rejections are an unfortunate but necessary means to a beautiful end. Every week you watch two people steadily falling into love."

"But if you read the front pages of the tabloids in the checkout line, only one season has led to a wedding. Seems to me the only place Love is leading these folks is face time on national television." Lia huffed and crossed her arms and legs.

Seemed like I was winning this argument. I smiled, leaned back into the cushions of the couch, and soaked in the rare victory. Lia got quiet. She gets quiet when she gets angry.

Which gets me talking, because I hate silence …

So in order to hammer home my point, I started to list off the seasons for Lia with my fingers while she sat with her arms crossed at me: "Let's see, the first stud was Alex, a Harvard grad, I believe, a lawyer with a slick smile. I could tell he was slimy from the first rose. You didn't see it, remember? There you sat, week after week, cooing on the couch as he kissed everybody. Then he dumped Trista at the last rose ceremony. Come on! She was awesome!

"The next year, that jock Aaron starred. He was like, 'I like you,' and the girl was like, 'I like you, too,' and he was like, 'Let's kiss,' and the girl was like, 'Okay.' It made me feel dirty. To your credit, Lia, you mostly took off watching that season.

"But then Trista came back, and you were hooked once again. We watched every episode, and it was awful. I mean, Trista was cool, but it was so obvious that Ryan was the best dude for her. They should have cut the season early and let the two live their life in peace. I was glad they got together, and they're Coloradans like us!

"The next season introduced Andrew Firestone, who was intriguing because of the tires, and he made wine or something. He wasn't that bad, and he made a wise choice in Jen. She was spunky.

"Following Firestone came Bachelor Bob. You loved that guy. 'He's so funny and sweet,' you always said. The girls were falling all over him, going gaga over his dimples and his perm. Frankly, I don't know what you all saw in him. Then, to top it off, Bob didn't choose Kelly Jo! By the end, if I recall, you were pretty ticked at Bachelor Bob too; it nearly broke your heart when he got rid of Meredith.

"I missed most of the next season when she was the Bachelorette, but I remember predicting that 'the guy with the floofy hair' would win as early as week two. And you wouldn't believe me.

"Then, the next season, I called it again—when New York Giant Jesse Palmer was the Bach, remember? That Jessica girl was very pretty. And Jesse didn't care that she was barely drinking age and in school on the other side of the country. You've got to respect that. He knew they were not getting married.

"Then ABC contracted Byron Somebody to be the next Bachelor. I admit he wasn't bad, either; after all, he was a pro bass fisherman, which may be the greatest profession there is. And he chose Mary—a wise choice. They may have a shot. I hope so.

"Then, the sacrilege: ABC moves *The Bach* to Monday night to lure us men who have set aside our Mondays for real reality television—which is called 'football'—with cool Jen, the girl Andrew Firestone chose but later dumped. They are so sneaky; they know they've cornered the market on female viewers, so they entice us with Jen and desecrate our night with 'the most surprising rose ceremony ever.' Those dogs! And then Jen drops the slammer on every single guy—even Jerry, the last man standing. What a show! It drives me bonkos to think they let this crap on television."

"We don't have to watch it if you don't want to," Lia said, once I was done.

"What?" I queried, surprised.

"We don't have to watch it, I said."

"You mean you'd give it up for me?"

"If you really feel that strongly, we can watch something else."

"But …" I said.

"But what?" answered Lia.

"But don't you want to check out Charlie, the new guy?"

"Nope. I don't need to if you don't."

"Well, I'll let you watch the first show and see if you like it."

She smiled. "When will you admit you are addicted to *The Bach*?"

I raised an eyebrow. "What an outrageous accusation!"

"You know more about the show than I do. I think you want to watch the first episode because you love *The Bachelor*."

"I love *The Bachelor*? How could you say such a thing?"

"Let's see, you've watched every season. You remember everything about it. I think those nights when I'm at the hospital and you 'watch it for me,' you are really watching for yourself."

"Lia, I watch *The Bach* because I know you like it. I can't believe you would accuse me of watching it for myself. For once, I try to do something nice, something sacrificial, and you throw it in my face."

"Fine. I don't want to watch Charlie. Let's do something else."

I felt my heart squeeze. "But …"

What a wuss; I'm such a girly man. Arnold would be ashamed. The only sacrilege is me. That Lia can love a "man" (if I can still call myself one) shows her ability to overlook obvious flaws (the only reason I had a shot with her in the first place).

That said, I confess: I love *The Bachelor*. I watch every rose ceremony I can. I visit the website to find out what happened on the episodes I miss. I'd even watch it over *Monday Night Football* (as long as the game is out of hand).

What can I say? I love love. I mean, how can you not love a love story?

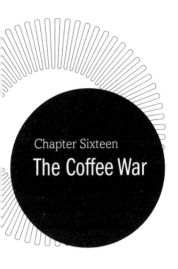

Lady Astor: If I were your wife, I would put poison in your coffee.
Winston Churchill: And if I were your husband I would drink it.[6]

Pascal, the French mathematician and philosopher, famously wrote that all mankind was created with a God-shaped vacuum— that God, in all His divine wisdom, thought it best to design human beings to be incomplete, leaving in us an empty space that would need filling. In other words, when God handed us the puzzle pieces of our hearts, He withheld one—a piece in the shape of Himself.

True or false, it seemed God made Lia with a coffee-shaped vacuum as well—a mug-shaped one that fit in the cup holder of her car and had a spill-proof lid. Lia Simpson Erickson was destined to be a coffee addict. She was born into a caffeinated world and into a family of caffeine junkies. She was doomed. It was in the cards, if not in the genes.

Her grandfather, Gus, an avid amateur genealogist, has traced roots back beyond colonial times, a confluence of coffee lovers through the ages running like a river boldly blended and roasted dark. He himself chased down his cigarettes with the black stuff for forty years. In 1975, after his heart finally alerted him with "one heck of a wake-up call," he kicked the sticks for good. But java, the liquid of life—that habit has continued uninterrupted. He now chases the newspaper with it. It sits shotgun at his side as he writes emails to his grandchildren. It lubricates his joints as he supernaturally cares for Ruthy, his love. She was diagnosed with Alzheimer's about two years ago and is starting to forget who he is. It's enough to crack your heart wide open. She still remembers how to fix her coffee, though—cream and two sugars. Doubt that knowledge will ever go away.

Their son and Lia's father, Rich, the quintessential modern man of moderation, drinks only one cup a day; it is just that the cup has grown from eight ounces of Styrofoam percolated in a breakroom vat and tasting like cardboard rubber bands to a Venti from the café Bon Pain with an added shot or two of espresso. Watching him work a coffeemaker on Saturday morning is like watching a master at his art. He creates beverages of beauty, potent enough to knock the crusties from your eyes and curl the hairs on your toes.

I have concluded that the Simpson DNA must have a caffeine-deficient gene. It's the only way I can make sense of their dependence.

With that in mind, it was understandable that Lia would have an inclination toward the most popular drug on the planet. By the middle of medical school, she was well on her way to the national average of 3.5 cups a day. And to concretize the inevitability, Lia was a doctor, waist deep in residency, on call every fourth night, and working the more humane eighty-hour weeks the United States government had so mercifully mandated. Poor girl. She lived in a perpetual state of fatigue, a permanent condition of exhaustion, a profound fog.

Waking up routinely before six in the morning and working thirty hours straight every four days took a toll, especially on those who, like Lia, were certifiably not morning people. Overnight, she grew what I refer to as poofy eyes—you know, the type of eyes boxers get around the sixth or seventh round. Suffice it to say, Lia was at her least beautiful in the morning. But that's not all; there was her mouth. Sometime during the wee hours, an odorous fungus, a petri dish's dream, would fester and culture-ize on the top of her tongue. One direct hit of breath could send you straight to the mortuary. However, it was more than her breath and her looks that took on the nature of Swamp Thing.

The fungified funk in her mouth was only the residual of the intangible foulness that had taken up residence inside her body. Morning-Lia and Texas had something in common: don't mess with them. If Lia ever had the capability to kill, it would happen between five and seven in the morning. Needless to say, we didn't have much of a relationship before the morning brewing.

Lia got in the habit of starting her day with coffee. Every morning it was like a miracle: within seconds of her inaugural sip, even before the coffee had stopped swirling after its stirring, Lia my wife returned—the kinder, gentler, less murderous one. The one I loved. The metamorphosis was so marvelous Bruce Banner would be impressed.

If you don't believe in radical transformation, witness Lia pre- and post-coffee, and you will certainly change your mind.

Our morning routine went on like this for quite some time. The alarm would sound. We would turn on the light in the room, and Lia would grunt. She would turn at me and glare as if it were my fault she had to wake up this early. I would divert my eyes and scurry to the bathroom where I would blow my nose (it's so weird—even if I don't have a cold, I always have to blow my nose first thing). Then I'd jump in the shower and stay there until I calculated she was sitting down to breakfast and her java. I'd dry off, throw on some clothes, and get to the kitchen in time to kiss her goodbye as she walked to the door. I would sit down with my cran-raspberry fruit juice and read in peace, knowing I had successfully avoided another near-death encounter with my Swamp Spouse.

But the whole arrangement unsettled me. It was honestly dis-concerting that my wife was only pleasant to be around while she was on drugs. Even though caffeine had a positive effect on Lia, the fact that it modified her behavior seemed hazardous. Sooner or later, addiction was going to catch up to her. What if the caffeine jolt lessened its effect? There was no telling. She was meddling with a gateway drug; what if she walked through the door? The thought scared me. I mean, I was a loving husband, and loving husbands were sworn to protect their wives. Wasn't that one of the vows? What was I to do, stand by and watch my love slip into the jowls of dependence? Solemnly, I was thereby committed to saving my wife from the clutches of caffeine before it was too late.

———————————

"You're addicted," I blurted out one day in the car. (I save conflict for when I'm driving—Lia tends to hold back her punches as long as I'm steering and her life is in my hands.)

"To what?" she asked, clueless.

"To caffeine. It's a drug, and you are totally dependent on it."

"No, I'm not."

"See, you are. The first stage is denial."

"I'm not in denial."

"Yes, you are."

"Ned, there's no way to answer an accusation like that. If I say I am addicted, I'm admitting it; if I say I'm not, you accuse me of being in denial."

"Lia, I can't help the fact that you are in denial, but I can help you by confronting you with the facts."

"The facts!" She was getting ticked.

This was getting exciting.

"Look at the facts. You yourself told me that you go to bed thinking about how great your coffee is going to taste in the morning. Then you spend the morning dreaming about the Coke you are going to drink at lunch. Don't you think it is a little unhealthy to be so attracted to a drug?"

"Ned."

"I'm not finished! You don't see the bloodshot eyes, the get-out-of-my-way look you have when you're beelining it to Mr. Coffee every morning."

"Ned, you're exaggerating. You're just jealous that there is something I like that you don't."

"Jealous! I'm not jealous. I'm sad. I'm sad that my wife is blinded by addiction, that she is ensnared by a drug, that she is wasting her life away in subservience to a beverage if something isn't done."

"Oh my gosh, I can't believe you are saying this!"

"Lia, it's only because I care for you and am concerned about your well-being that I mention this at all," I snickered, as our car made a right-hand turn.

"Ned, listen to me. I'm not addicted. I just like it. Liking something is not wrong. Don't you want me to be able to enjoy things?"

"True, there is nothing wrong with liking something, but becoming dependent on a drink is not good."

"So what if I need it? I like it."

"Oh, so you're saying a cocaine addict can snort cocaine as long as he likes it?"

"Ned."

"I see, it's all right to be an alcoholic as long as he enjoys it. That makes sense."

"That's not what I'm saying. Coffee is different."

"The only difference is that coffee is legal and half the world is strung out on it. And the other half is afraid to say anything because of the violence that would ensue if you took their coffee away."

"Well, take the world's advice and let us all drink our coffee in peace."

I was loving it. I feigned frustration. I huffed, "I can't believe this. It's impossible to reason with people like you. Maybe you are right; maybe I should keep my mouth shut. You are so far over the edge, Leela. I'm not sure it's even possible to bring you back."

"I'm going to drink coffee whether you like it or not," Lia huffed back. She pivoted away from me and toward the passenger window, the position she assumes during car conflicts when she has had enough.

Conversation and Round One over—I'd have to say I won.

So you can imagine my surprise when, last November, Lia told me over dinner that she was quitting coffee for the month of December.

"I told you! You were addicted. I was right, wasn't I?" I couldn't believe it. A marriage first! Mark down this date; Lia had heeded a warning of mine. Lia had actually listened to advice from her husband's mouth and had taken it to heart. I swelled in triumph.

(How soon we get deflated.)

She put down her fork and looked at me with a what-gave-you-that-idea glare. "Ned, I'm not giving it up for you. I'm taking a break because I've been noticing that the coffee's powers are not as potent as they used to be. I've got a light month at the hospital and figured if I quit drinking for a while, the old zing will return when I start up again."

"What?" I said in disbelief.

"My tolerance has gotten too high. So I'm giving my body a month to lose the tolerance I've built up."

"Basically, you just want the old buzz back," I said, understanding. "You are so addicted. I thought you were stopping because I had influenced you."

Lia stared at me across the table. "Dream on, big boy."

That did it. She had called me "big boy." Where I come from, them's fightin' words. Come hell or high water, I was going to tempt her into breaking her fast. I was going to prove, once and for all, that my bride was an addict.

The Coffee War had begun.

Looking back, it was a foolish play on my part. If I really believed she was suffering under caffeine's dominion, I should have encouraged her, supported her, held her hand, and cheered her on.

No dice. It was game time. I sent Logic packing and cloaked my intentions in Passionate Insanity. I put on my pads, grabbed my helmet, and went headlong into a no-huddle offense. Sometimes being right is more important than doing right. The truth was, I didn't want Lia to quit; I wanted her to lose.

So I decided to start drinking coffee myself.

Oh what tangled webs we weave, when first we practice to deceive! Cut the irony with a knife and serve me a double portion, please. What was I thinking?

I don't know. It seemed like a good idea. *Simple exposure will trigger the impulse*, I thought. *Mere locality will do the trick. If I make the substance available, she won't be able to resist the temptation. All I have to do is partake—poison myself, just a little.* It was a foolish strategy, but it felt right at the time.

Falling into Love

And so, I added coffee-making to my pre-bed routine. I'd mosey over to the fridge, open the metal magnet door, and rotate the butter window (where we kept our coffee at the time). I'd unzip the ziploc and unlock the aroma. I would sniff the disk on the front of the package with eyes closed and mouth smiling, then undo the tabs, unroll, and sniff again at the opening. With a hand I'd waft the scent toward Lia and wait for a reaction. I would start making *mmm*ing moans of increasing volume and wait again. I would lick my finger and stick it in the package. I would carry the crystals to bed and rub them into her pillowcase ... to stimulate her neurons into a frenzy while she slept.

In the morning I would drink my first cup of the day. I made it bold; I made it strong. I drank it as we read next to each other, and then I placed it between us (a little closer to Lia every time). I would mention, as if to the heat ventilator, "My, what a wonderful blend. This might be the best cup yet."

Nonchalantly, with not-so-innocent intention, I'd ask, "Do you want to take a sip?" (as if I had forgotten her commitment).

Lia ignored me, but I knew she wanted some.

"One sippy? Two sippy? Four sippy? Oops, Mississippi!"

She didn't laugh. She took a gulp of her cranraspberry juice and continued to work on her crossword.

"You'd be a lot better at crossword puzzles if you drank coffee," I suggested.

She chewed the end of her pen and pretended I didn't exist.

"Come on, Leela. I need your opinion on this coffee, since you're an expert and all. Tell me if you think it is too weak."

Lia propped her chin with a palm pedestal.

"How about a whiff? Just a whiffy?"

She plugged her ear with her middle finger.

"Am I getting under your skin? You're breaking, aren't you?"

I gave her a week before she'd cave. It was only a matter of time.

That's how Lia must have looked at it, too. One of her strongest qualities is her willpower. Her spirit is so strong that if it were translated into coffee, she would be a triple espresso to the tenth power. Her will is Herculean.

All month she remained steadfast. She didn't bend—not on any of the twelve days of Hanukkah; not on Christmas Eve or Christmas Day; not on the frozen, frosty mornings or on the foggy, groggy afternoons—not on any day at all. By January 1, Lia had sufficiently completed her self-imposed detoxification program. As the finish line approached, I could make out a coffee bean gleam in her eye.

As for me, I believe it was the aroma that first enraptured me. I was wrong about the best smell. Coffee Smell beats Man Smell, hands down. Its grains are a pixie dust of lust.

I drank at least a cup every day in December. And I'm not sure which day it happened; I'm not sure if it was in the first week. But I'm sure it happened before December 12, the night I came to the horrific realization that we were out of coffee.

It was ten o'clock. I approached the fridge as usual, opened the metal magnet door, and rotated the butter window. The coffee sack felt light. I had known we were getting low. Granules shifted. I took my now-habitual whiff, then scooped what I could—enough to turn the water brown, but not enough to satisfy. I had to make a split-second decision: go to the store tonight, or treat myself to Starbucks in the morning (to forgo was not an option.)

Why not both? I thought. *What's the point in choosing?*

"I'll be right back!" I shouted down the hall to an already sleeping Leela, and out the door I went.

Well, at least I got one thing right: caffeine is a drug. I now know firsthand. I am an addict. So is Lia, though she still won't admit it. Napoleon is quoted as having said, "I would rather suffer with coffee than be senseless."[7] My sentiments exactly—it seems Napoleon and I share more in common than lack of height.

So now I prepare coffee for two. Lia likes hers with half-and-half; I like mine with milk and sugar.

Being a druggie isn't as bad as I thought it would be. The way I see it, caffeine is something that brings us together, something that helps fill the empty places inside—something that neither of us will do without again.

"Leela, at precisely what time did we leave our planet and land on this one?"

"I don't know. I haven't seen an exit sign in an hour."

"Me neither. What happens if we get low on gas?"

"Let's pray we don't find out. Maybe we should stop at the next station and fill up, to be on the safe side."

"You mean, *if* there's a next one. I'm not sure anyone lives here anymore."

"In Utah?" asked Lia.

"I think they all moved."

"I bet property value is pretty cheap out here."

"Hey, let's buy some! I bet we could buy a thousand acres for five bucks."

"Let's not, and say we did," said Lia, just in case I was serious.

"I wonder if Orrin Hatch ever spends time campaigning out here. I don't even see a cow."

"Who's Orrin Hatch?"

"He's Utah's senator, I think."

"Oh."

"If voter turnout is strong, you're still only talking like fifteen people."

"How many people *do* live out here?" Lia asked.

"The real question is, how many people *did* live here? I don't think anybody does now."

"Don't know why. I think it's kind of beautiful."

"What's beautiful?" I asked.

"The scenery. I love how you can see so far in the distance. I love those mesas on our right—makes you want to go horseback riding, doesn't it? If Lake Powell is as pretty as this ... I wonder how warm the water's going to be."

"From the looks of our surroundings, my guess is they drained it," I replied.

It was August, and we were driving toward the two-hundred-mile canyon-walled Lake Powell, which did look breathtaking from the pictures we had seen online. It was filled from the north by the Colorado River and retained a couple hundred miles later by the Glen Canyon Dam. It was the second-largest manmade lake in the United States and one of the warmest, clearest bodies of water within driving distance of Denver. Since moving to Colorado earlier that summer, we had hiked and fished and climbed as much as we could. But by August, we were missing the Carolina coast. We had tossed around the idea of flying back, but the timing hadn't worked out, and the Atlantic was a bit too far for a weekend road trip. Lake Powell would have to suffice. So that's where we were heading—at least that's where I thought we were heading. I hadn't seen a hint of water since Grand Junction.

Eastern Utah, if you have never been there, is a vast expanse of tumbleweed, sedimentary rock, and dirt. The speed limit is seventy-five, and yellow signs warn of windstorms. We eventually did come across a town, about one hundred miles west of the border. All we remember is its name: Green River. Well, that, and it might own the record for most hotels per capita. We counted twenty-six on the way to get gas. (We filled up, just to be safe.)

The atmosphere in our four-wheeled chariot was quite comfortable. We had a full supply of gas; I was even using the air conditioner, something I rarely do. Still a couple of hours away from where the map told us Lake Powell should be, I slowly eased the car into cruise control, and we sped into nothing once again.

Lia turned on the radio and hit the seek button. The digits flew by, finally stopping on a country station to her liking. She started singing along with the Dixie Chicks, a song containing a slew of "ready's." She gave me a tender glance and harmonized with Natalie Maines: "What's all this talk about luhhhhhh ..."

I couldn't make out the last word—something like "us" or "lust" or "love" or "lunch." I have always been poor at lyrics, a personal idiosyncrasy that causes Lia to patronize (or is it matronize, if it comes from a woman?).

Just last week at dinnertime, I slid in some music to chew by, as is our custom, and began bobbing to the beat of Bob Marley's *Legend*. I swayed my arms like a dreadlock in the breeze and sang to Lia with all my heart and soul. "I don't want no wedding day for your love!" I grabbed her hips and forced them to click like a clock to the timing of the bass drum. "I don't want no wedding day for your love," I sang again.

"I *thought* that's what you said," Lia said with a quizzical gleam.

"What's what I said?" I asked.

"You sang, 'I don't want no wedding day for your love.'"

Sensing a lyric battle, I justified my rationale: "Yeah. You know, I am so in love with you, I can't wait until our wedding day to be with you."

"Ned, the real words are 'I don't want to wait in vain for your love.'"

"You want to bet?"

"Dishes for a week."

"You're on. Course, I'm gonna have to teach you how to do them," I said.

We walked over to the case to settle the argument. She was right. Bob didn't want to wait in vain.

"Well, I don't care how the liner notes read. When Bob sings through my stereo, he sings 'wedding day.'"

Lia tossed me the scrub brush.

What can I say? I have bad ears. I wonder if that's why I have such difficulty listening sometimes. I'm handicapped. Maybe Lia would take it easier on me if she knew I was disabled.

By pure luck, I punched the dial and landed on the greatest road trip song of all time: "Jessica," by the Allman Brothers. I bounced in my seat with delight and smiled over at Lia, who was doing her best to hide her enthusiasm but was smiling. I could tell.

I decided to make a game of it. "Okay, Leela, here's the deal. We'll take turns singing along to songs on the radio. If we can sing most of the lyrics to a song, we gets five points. If we can't, we can press the seek button for a one-point reduction."

"What if the next station is on a commercial break?" Lia asked.

"You have to hit seek again. Who wants to listen to commercials?"

"So I have five points, right?"

"Sure, whatever."

Now, I don't want to toot my own horn, but as bad as I am with lyrics, it's a whole different ball game when it comes to instrumental songs. For some reason, I immediately internalize every layer and nuance. What is that, a phonographic memory? Whatever it is, I have it. Sweet old "Jessica" has oodles of onion-like tracks to be enjoyed. And I knew every one by heart. I tapped the steering wheel and, right alongside Dickey Betts, sang, "Dah-dah-dah-dat-doo-dah-dah-dat-doo-dah-dah-dah-dee ..."

Lia rarely appreciates the finer things, like a great guitar solo or the way a cigarette butt makes mini fireworks when it alights on a road at night. She wasn't impressed. She smiled to be nice—the equivalent of patting Chelsea on the head when she's being annoying.

"Five points for me," I said as the song crescendoed to an end.

She blew a breathful of air up her face. "That song didn't have any lyrics."

"So?" I said.

"You said you'd get five points if you knew most of the lyrics," Lia said.

"Let's play by the spirit of the law, not the letter, please. I have five points; you know it."

"Actually, you have four points because you hit the seek button."

"Leela," I said, getting mad. I hate losing.

Lia smiled. "My turn," she said.

"Take out the paper and the trash ..." boomed through the speakers.

"Or you don't get no spending cash," sang Lia. Her shoulders moved to the beat; she had a Betty Boop bat to her eyelashes. God, was she pretty.

By the sax solo, the cuteness of my bride, combined with The Coasters' "Yakety Yak," diffused all anger about being behind in the game.

Leela looked like she'd been yakety yakking since 1958, which is near impossible when you're twenty-six years old. She sang like it was her favorite song.

"Don't talk back," she croaked.

And we both erupted into laughter. Leela sounded like a frog singing a Barry White song.

By the last *yak* I was in fine spirits. I turned off the radio and improvised a verse of my own:

> We are driving down the road ... bom bom bah da bom bom
> Hoping the lake ain't overflowed ... bom bom bah da bom bom
> Or else we turn into a toad ... bom bom bah da bom bom
> I wonder if my lawn got mowed ... yakety yak
> ("Don't talk back," croaked Leela)

"Hey, do you have a slice of gum?" I asked. "I think this Utah desert is evaporating my saliva."

Lia reached into her purse and produced.

"Thank you, my love." I batted my eyes and made a kissy face that I think is so cute.

She half smiled and turned the radio back on.

Hall and Oats came over the airwaves: "Because your kiss is on my lips," I sang toward Lia.

"Ned, it's 'kiss is on my list.' On my *list*! Not on my *lips*!"

"Nah, can't be. It doesn't make sense: your kiss is on my list?"

"It's because your kiss is on my list of the best things in life," sang Lia.

"No, no, no," I corrected, "it's because your kiss is on my lips when we make out tonight."

Lia sighed. "You're not funny, and I'm not talking about this anymore."

"I wasn't trying to be funny," I lied. "I guess we'll just have to agree to disagree." I continued to munch on my gum and internally hum.

The sky was as blue as the Utah desert was brown, without a cloud to behold. We were both quiet, silently watching the white lane markers clip by.

As the minutes passed, it became apparent that something was unnerving Lia. She shifted left; she shifted right. She could not get comfortable. She fiddled with the air conditioner. That wasn't it. The Romantics' "What I Like About You" was fading into static; our game had lost momentum. She turned the radio off. A second later she switched it back on, hit the seek button, and the radio circumnavigated the airwaves without landing anywhere. She turned it off again.

Maybe she has to pee, I thought. *Girls and their peeing* ... Out of compassion I set the cruise control one mile an hour faster.

I folded my hands behind my head and drove with my knee until finally Lia couldn't take it anymore: "Ned, do you know that you chew gum with your mouth open?" she asked.

"What?" What was she talking about?

"You sound like our dog."

"Chelsea doesn't chew gum," I said.

Lia huffed. "When you chew gum, you sound like our dog." She smacked her lips to give me an audio example.

"Huh?"

"And you look like a cow. Basically, you're an animal."

"I thought you had to pee."

"Huh? I don't have to pee. I just can hardly think with all your smacking going on."

"Hey, those are mean words," I said. All of a sudden, my chest felt kind of weird. I think I was beginning to have hurt feelings.

Lia didn't notice or care. She continued to complain: "Actually, you chew everything with your mouth open."

"So?"

"So, you are so loud I can't even concentrate. You drive me crazy."

"It can't drive you *that* crazy," I reasoned.

"Oh, yes it does."

"If it bothered you that much, why haven't you said anything before now?"

"I don't know. I thought I would be able to tolerate it."

"Lia, we've been married for three years, and you've never mentioned this before."

"I figured it would eventually bother you as much as it bothers me."

I was confused and needed clarification: "So you are saying that for three years and more than one thousand meals, you have been slowly going insane by the way I chew?" I was close to losing my temper.

"Yep," said Lia.

Now, I don't get angry often, but my very nature was being called into question. I raised my voice. "Lia, I like the way I chew. It's worked for me for twenty-eight years without a hitch, without a single person correcting me. I think you are the one with the problem. As far as I'm concerned, I chew great. I'm an excellent chewer. I've never choked, not even on a chunk of steak. My incisors can obliterate the meanest hunks of meat. My bicuspids can cut the stalest, sturdiest loafs of bread to smithereens. Don't even get me started on my molars. They're like jackhammers! I'm a natural! That's right; no one ever had to teach me how to chew."

"Well, maybe someone should have," said Lia.

Ouch. That smarted. What's worse, I couldn't think of anything mean to say back.

Do I really have a problem? Have people been laughing at me behind my back, saying things like: "Have you seen that Ned guy graze? Didn't his mama ever teach him anything? Do you think he does it on purpose?" Maybe my eating technique is poor … that would explain why I never could hold down a steady girlfriend, why so many girls mysteriously broke up with me. They were scared away by my fangs.

I took a different tack: "Oh, Lia. It can't be that bad."

"Ned, please just stop chewing with your mouth open. It's killing me."

"Fine," I said.

I obediently started moving my jaw up and down in lip-lock position. It felt awkward and new and strange. The silence was deafening.

Inside, I was boiling. Lia had wounded me deeply. Nothing hurts as bad as having someone point out a flaw you didn't know you had. It was a painful blow. It made me hot. I wanted to retaliate. At least, part of me did. The other part wanted me to cut my losses—who knew what else Lia might bring up?

But I hadn't been this angry in a long time. And we were in a car in the middle of nowhere. If I was ever going to fight for my dignity, this was the time and the place to do it. I picked up a grievance grenade and chucked it: "Lia, I didn't want to say this, but there are lots of things that you do that drive me nuts. In my opinion, it is more honorable to keep quiet about them. In fact, I simply chalk them up as endearing qualities."

It was a bluff. Frankly, nothing Lia did irked me. She's about as perfect a woman as there is.

But my comment seemed to do the trick. I was on the offense now. Confident, I gripped the steering wheel and changed lanes, just because I could.

Lia was taken aback. "Tell me. What do I do that is annoying?" she asked disbelievingly.

"Lots of things."

"Name one," she challenged.

Shoot. She had called my bluff. I had to think fast. What did Lia do that ticked me off? Nothing. Was there anything Lia did that was annoying? Nope. There had to be some bad habit I could exploit. There had to be something. This stunk. My obliviousness and lack of observation were catching up to me. I cursed my go-with-the-flow nature. I had thought it was an asset; it turned out to be my bane.

I looked over at Lia, searching for a clue.

She looked back. "I'm waiting."

"Give me a second," I retorted, "I'm trying to pick which one to mention. It's hard when there are so many." I looked out the window. *God, help. Give me something ... anything ... please!*

Then, all of a sudden, as if He were listening, God gave ... and Lia blew her nose.

I think I had noticed Lia's unique style of nose-blowing before, yet I can't remember ever truly analyzing it. Granted, no one blows his or her nose with particular grace, but Lia's style takes the cake. Let me try to describe it: she starts normally enough; she places the tissue in her hands, cradles her nose, and jettisons—nothing particularly noteworthy. Then, just before expulsion is complete, Lia takes her two index fingers and sticks them up her nose! Hidden from sight, clothed in a white tissue gown like two ghostly Halloweeners going door to door for tricks and treats, she rotates her fingers in clockwise circles until she is convinced that all mucus has been sufficiently expunged. Then, to top it all off, after she unplugs her nostrils, she looks at the result: two reverse dimples like fawn horns protruding for all the world to see.

I sat there watching my bride, this same woman who moments earlier had denounced my trivial habit of chewing gum with my mouth open. I watched my wife, Lia Erickson, MD, stick both fingers up her nose, roll them all around, pull them out, and inspect them for carnage. I mean, gross is gross, but that is *gross*!

"Oh, yeah," I said with confidence, "you want to know what you do that's completely repulsive? Let's examine the way you blow your nose."

"My nose?" Lia asked incredulously.

"Yeah, your nose. Take a look at that poor tissue you just obliterated. You see those two little horns?"

Lia looked with little regard.

"Those two bumps are from your fingers, which you stick up your nose every time you blow it!"

"What's wrong with that? Doesn't everybody do it that way?"

"No. You're the only one I've ever seen do it that way." I took the wheel with my knee and began mimicking with my free hands.

I must have looked funny because Lia started laughing.

"It's sanitary nose picking, that's all," I said, mimicking again after seeing the smile it put on her face. In Lia voice, I continued, "I just want to make sure I get all of it out."

Lia laughed harder.

"Oh," I looked down at my two fingers, "how cute! Two inverted dimples. Makes me want to tweak them ... I love little dimples!"

Lia laughed herself into convulsions. When Lia laughs, she uses her entire body. Tears began streaming down her cheeks; snot began flowing down her philtrum.

"Need a tissue?" I asked and rotated my fingers underneath my nose in mockery. I couldn't keep my laughter in either. I let out a gigantic guffaw, and my gum shot forth from my mouth, landing on the dashboard. Tears welled in my eyes, and I could feel the car beginning to drift.

"Ned, stop!" cried Lia in between giggles. She grabbed my knee affectionately. "You are going to get us into an accident."

She was probably right, but it was hard to gain composure. I concentrated on slowing my breathing down and finally got control of our car. We eased back on the road and took deep breaths.

"I love you," I said with all my heart and soul.

"I love you, too," she said with meaning.

"I think the way you blow your nose is actually kind of cute, in a gross kind of way."

"I still think you chew like a barnyard animal," replied Lia.

"Thanks."

"Don't mention it."

I regained my launched gum and inspected; it was covered in dash dust. I thought about it, but then thought better.

"Hey," I said, batting my eyes in my ever-so-adorable way, "do you mind getting me another slice of gum?"

"Let's just listen to the radio."

Chapter Eighteen
Newlywed Game

I love cruises. I've only been on one, but it sold me. What was it, exactly? The destinations? (Those islands, like shocks of Chia Pet hair rising in protuberance over the silk sheets of aquamarine and turquoise, blanketing a waterbed world of porpoises, kaleidoscopic fish, and Galapagos turtles.) The food? (The guarantee of twenty-four-hour buffet lines the size of a flatbed trailer, when the choice between filet mignon and lobster tail is both.) The mornings? (When you begin another crystal Caribbean day with a few laps around the upper deck; a breakfast of salami on a croissant, with a side of mango and cottage cheese; and thirty minutes of Jazzercise—all before nine o'clock.) The nights? (When an evening consists of dinner followed by theater, five games of ping-pong, trivia at the Skybar, a failed attempt to go under hypnosis, and wailing away to "Livin' on a Prayer" at the karaoke lounge.) Need I go on?

When I picture heaven, I picture a cruise—everything provided, all expenses paid.

Lia and I had joined the Simpson family for a spring break cruise. We had excitedly awaited the trip for months, eager to spend time in the water and with family. We had found only two drawbacks to living in Colorado: the lack of water and the long distance to Ohio, where Lia was from, and Pennsylvania, where I was from. This trip would remedy both.

Each night, Lia and I would enter our sarcophagus of a room and fight for the one-page bulletin that had been *whish*ed under our door while we were out catching a comedian or playing a late-night game of canasta. The one-page newsletter segmented the next day into fifteen-minute increments, indicating each block's events. We'd belly-flop to the mattress, complimentary pen in hand, and circle activities, making the tough decision between bingo on the poop deck and ballroom dancing in the Swan Room. By the time we said good night, our entire next day was planned. Our daily bulletin of little circles looked like a Scantron. We'd close our eyes and hope our marks held the answers to another great day.

But as high as our nightly expectations were, nothing prepared us for what happened. How could we have guessed that one of those circles would lay the groundwork for one of the greatest moments of our marriage?

We plopped on the bed after another nonstop day-o-fun—our third straight, I recall. Lia unfolded the next day's schedule and began perusing the events with her finger. I lifted the pen from the nightstand, ready. Every few centimeters she'd pause, circling with her finger the merengue lessons she wanted to take. I'd cement the decision with the pen.

She continued down the page: 10:00 Lagoon Lounge—The Newlywed Game.

Her finger bounced with glee.

"Double-circle that baby," she chirped.

"Heck, yeah! I'm putting an asterisk beside that bad boy!"

She beamed at me. "We're gonna win, aren't we?"

"Darn right, we are."

We shook hands like we were sealing a deal.

"Tomorrow," Lia told me, "let's go find who is in charge and make sure we can be contestants."

"Sounds like a plan."

So the next day, between the *Jock Jams* step class and a puppet presentation of *Gulliver's Travels*, we picked up a contestant question-naire from the event coordinator lady and skipped the puppets so we could concentrate on writing quality answers.

The sheet asked how long we had been married. We answered three years, eight months, twelve days, nineteen hours, twenty-six minutes, and counting. They asked how we met. We wrote a short story about the Brownie Bet. They asked about our biggest fight. We wrote about my loud gum-chewing. They asked why they should choose us. I tried to convince Lia to lie and say that one of us had terminal cancer. Lia thought we should write something about how we would throw ourselves overboard if we weren't selected. We ended up signing "Please!" and leaving it at that.

Later that afternoon, we hunted down Event Coordinator Lady. I handed over our document like it was the Magna Carta; we begged before her like a dog. I started saying something about "gangli-onic parapsycho carcinoma" but got elbowed in the kidneys, so it sounded more like "garchhk."

Event Coordinator Lady lifted an eyebrow but dismissed it as a cough, or maybe a hairball. Regardless, she didn't inquire. She wore makeup and jingly earrings.

Lia thanked her for her thoughtful consideration of our ap-plication and bowed. Event Coordinator Lady wouldn't promise anything but told us to be ready and present tonight.

"Do you think we have a shot?" asked Lia as we walked along the promenade.

"Well, I don't know. But I think I caught her winking at us."

"Oh, I do hope we're chosen."

My stomach dropped. What if we *were* chosen? It had been fun thinking about being onstage, but being asked funny questions about our personal life in front of hundreds of strangers and my family-in-law? In-laws!

Lia's parents would be in the audience! I loved them and knew they loved me, but how would they feel after I told the world how often I made whoopee with their first daughter? I could see Rich's expression now—here he comes, cracking his knuckles, asking me if I want to see the five of clubs! The man would kill me.

Lia has told me that stress does not create ulcers, but I felt one beginning to barnacle itself to my stomach lining. For the first time, I could sense the ship's sway. Was I getting seasick? I sure wasn't feeling well. Frantically, I checked the railing—if I jumped, would I die on impact or would I have to wait for the sharks to get me? Either option seemed more pleasant than full disclosure before the in-laws.

It was hard to concentrate during merengue class; I could hardly eat my cordon bleu and crab cakes during dinner. The closer "the game" approached, the more nervous I became.

I wondered how Lia was feeling. Maybe she was as nervous as I was. Maybe she was feigning enthusiasm. Maybe she was just waiting for me to make the first move, to suggest tracking down Event Coordinator Lady and scratching our names from the list. I had to find out.

So pulling her aside after dinner, I asked, "What if they choose us, Lia?"

"We'll win," she asserted with confidence.

"No, what if they ask us something embarrassing?"

"Ned, you never get embarrassed."

"But what if they ask us about having …" I whispered, "sex?"

"Who cares?"

"Lia, your parents will be watching!"

"They don't care."

"How do you know that?"

She just did; nothing was changing her mind.

"Ned, if you screw this up," she warned in a stern voice, "I'll kill you."

Dead if I do, dead if I don't. I gulped, "For the record, I don't think this is a good idea. I vote to watch the magician instead." (Little did I know real magic was going to happen that night.)

————————

The Lagoon Lounge had round, polished oak tables and candle-lamp centerpieces. The ceiling was colored glass, a bluish-green pond with lily pads like frog hands and pink flowers like baby bellybuttons. It gave the room a murky glow. We entered like salmon, the whole Simpson entourage swimming to a balcony-eddy large enough to hold us all: Rich and Sue, Cara, Caitlin, Chad, and Lia and me. They all seemed excited.

Aloof, I leaned back on two legs of my chair, scouting for a waitress and some hard liquor. Lia stood above me, too excited to sit down, scouting for the eye of Event Coordinator Lady. We hadn't talked much since our last conversation. Lia was going to play if she had to play by herself (which I don't think was permissible).

I touched the loose skin on her elbow. She recoiled—if I didn't want to play, she didn't want anything to do with me. How many couples stayed married after appearing on *The Newlywed Game*? I wondered. This one wasn't going to survive without it! I watched my wife search the side stages. Lia was always beautiful, but there were moments when I noticed it more than others. Tonight she was radiant.

I admired the profile of her face. Her mouth was wet and slightly open, her teeth peeking like pearls in an oyster. Her eyes sparkled in the artificial ether. How similar were the elements of space and sea! What mystery; what knowledge! She could be a celestial angel; she could be a mermaid siren.

I traced the line of her slender sternomastoid (I missed our med school anatomy lab dates) to where it attached to her irregular right clavicle—the bone that had healed like a bend in a river after she broke it as a young teenager, falling from her stumbling horse. It was the same fall that had knocked out her front tooth, which had been replaced by the one that shines dull in black light. She was wearing a dress the color of a sea anemone, the strap inconspicuously hiding the bump. And as I recalled the history of her clavicle, I ached at how little I knew about the history of her heart underneath. How much I loved this woman, yet how little of her I knew! How could we win a game that measures understanding? Had I ever discerned a thought, a feeling, an intention? I had to be the dumbest husband on the globe.

How does Lia live with me? How have we made it this long? Three years, six months, thirteen days, five hours, fifty-eight minutes, and counting … I chuckled at the thought. Well, there was one thing I knew: Lia wanted to play. I might not know anything else, but I did know that. I looked again at Lia, my little mini pumpkin. My chest beat with love, and I made up my mind. How could I not play? Win or lose, I would give my all.

I stood up beside her, pulled back the hair over her ear, and hooked it behind like a curtain. "Let's go find the lady."

"Are you in?" she asked.

"All the way," I said.

I couldn't remember ever seeing her so happy.

She took my hand, and we took one step—but it was too late. The lights suddenly dimmed, save for a bright one aimed at a man in a white tuxedo. He walked up to the center stage microphone and welcomed the spectators with some indecipherable chatter. He slipped his fingers between his jacket and shirt, pulling out a sheet containing "the four lucky couples."

The first names belonged to Chuck and Betsy, who had been married yesterday in the ship's chapel by the captain. I squeezed Lia's hand. Our eyes locked.

White Tuxedo Man called the next names—ours.

We had been selected. We embraced and ran into the spotlight. The other two couples were veterans, one literally so—Larry and Mae were veterans of World War II and had been married for more than fifty years. The other marriage veterans were an odd couple by the names of Ray and Belinda. They were wearing matching tie-dyes and celebrating their thirtieth anniversary.

We shook hands with everyone, just like in my favorite scene from the movie *Spies Like Us*, where Chevy Chase and Dan Aykroyd play fake doctors. In the presence of these couples, these Marriage MDs, I felt like the fake.

What does marriage feel like, anyway? The silver on my ring finger looked unnatural to me, and I still played with it incessantly like a marital rookie. It was a wonder I hadn't lost it yet.

They sent Chuck, Larry, Ray, and me outside; the girls would be asked the first round of questions, and we'd guess the answers.

The men made small talk out in the hall. I quietly scanned their faces. I was the youngest by far but sensed we were all equals in apprehension. In chorus, we complained that our spouses had dragged us into this, but deep down we all knew we were joking. I remembered my double circle the night before. Was I any different from these guys, or were we all the same?

Event Coordinator Lady walked her high-heeled pumps over

to us and led us back to our women, who were all smiles, holding poster board placards blank side up. The answers were on the back.

As I sat beside Lia, she grabbed my hand and winked.

Here we went ...

First question: what is your pet name for your spouse? The first name that came to mind was Leela. *No, that's a nickname, not a pet name*, I told myself. *Have Lia and I talked about this? What if she doesn't know the difference?* Well, I had to say something. *I'll go with the truth.*

Tuxedo Man directed the question at me. I said, "In honor of Jackie, our first pumpkin, and her little children: little mini pumpkin."

She revealed her answer.

Ten points!

After the first round, everyone was tied.

Second question: where was your first kiss? I thought about answering "on the lips," and inadvertently laughed aloud at my cleverness. Lia read my mind and gave me the eyebrow V of death. I answered, "At Stone Mountain, in a creek," almost adding how it was truly a first kiss. But I decided against it.

We had twenty points.

Third question: what's the first thing you touch in the morning? *Whoa, that's a toughie.* I thought hard. What would Lia say? The only thing that came to mind was the first thing she usually complained about.

I said, "My nose when I blow it."

Lia revealed her card. It said "my lips." She shrugged. We had understood the question differently; she had thought about the first thing I touch on her. But Lia's answer would have nevertheless been wrong. I don't kiss her for a long time in the morning—she's got swamp breath, and it's dangerous to get too close to her, pre-coffee.

Good thing everyone else got it wrong, too. We were tied for the lead.

Fourth question, multiple choice: who do you hate the most? (A) one of your spouse's friends, (B) one of your spouse's co-workers, (C) a member of your spouse's family, or (D) other.

Aw, man. I had no idea what Lia would say. I had no idea what I would say. I felt the spotlights getting hotter. I just couldn't decide. I loved all of Lia's friends, I loved the folks she worked with, and I loved her family (not to mention they were sitting in the crowd). I genuinely believed in the goodness of man and that love really could conquer all. I could not think of a man, woman, or child I had ever met whom I didn't love at some level or doubted loved me back. Even the Ned-Haters League. After all, I married the president. Honestly, I loved everybody!

So that's what I said: "Well, I'm going out on a limb here. I'll have to say (E) no one. I love everybody!"

As the words came from my mouth, the entire place went nuts. For the first time I realized how many people were watching. Folks were sharing stools at the bar and resting shoulder blades on the wall. There were maybe five hundred people, and they were all cheering. Why? I must have done something embarrassing. I shifted uneasily and thought about how to check my fly without being obvious.

Searchingly, I besought Lia's face for a clue. She was beaming from ear to ear. When she flipped her answer over, I knew why. It read, "He loves everybody!"

We had both answered E!

The lounge erupted in hysterics—hoots, hollers, handclaps, the whole nine yards. I jumped to my feet and raised my arms like Rocky. Lia laid aside her sign and put her arms around my waist. Why had I been afraid?

Without any warning, in the twinkling of an eye, like magic, we had just experienced one of the greatest moments of our marriage.

I sat back down and hugged my dear, sweet Leela.

"Can you believe it?" I whispered in her ear.

"Yes, I can. I love you," she said.

The competition wasn't over, but it was clear we were the champs.

The rest of the game went by in a blur. It didn't even matter that they asked about the craziest place we had ever made love (easy question—we've only made love in one crazy place; it was either there or a bed). It didn't even matter that we ended up losing. Oh, well. We were all winners, I guess. At least Tuxedo Man gave us all a bottle of champagne. As Lia and I walked to our seats, we were greeted and treated like heroes. People were slapping us on the back and shaking our palms; one guy tousled my hair. Lia's family was all hugs and kisses. Rich's expression was one of pride and elation.

The rest of the cruise, we felt like celebrities. Lia and I'd be walking across the deck, towels slung over our shoulders, and feel people talking about us. We would overhear a woman in a lounge chair telling her husband how sweet a couple we were. Strangers would pass by and say, "Look! The Newlywed couple," or "Hey, it's Mr. I-Love-Everybody!"

I ate it up like salami croissants for breakfast.

When do you stop being newlyweds? Lia and I are going on five years and wondering when it will end—the newlywed feeling. Is that good? Or bad? When will we figure this marriage thing out? As I think back, our entire marriage has been a series of stumbles, falls, and guesses. Every once and a while, like on the cruise ship, I step out on a limb and guess correctly. But just as often, the branch breaks, and I fall flat on my face. Lia and I have no idea what we're doing. We have no clue where our life together will lead.

When it comes down to it, marriage is a journey with no trail, no map, and no destination. At best, marriage is an educated guess.

Are we the only ones who feel like this? Or do you feel it too?

On your wedding day, did you stand before a priest and make absurd promises you would never be able to keep, like we did? Did you stand across from a person you only partially knew—where the part you knew best was the good part, and the part you knew least was the bad, the real? And you rashly pledged undying love. You stood in a fog of hormones and idealism, vainly believing that when the clouds receded, the yellow brick road of happiness would take you far from wicked witches and lead you to a wizard in an emerald city who knew the way home. Didn't you?

In reality, when the fog lifted, the two of you quickly discovered not only that there was no clear road, but that there were no clear signs either. There was very little light at all, and what was visible did not look promising.

Or are Lia and I alone in feeling this way?

Who can predict a happy marriage? Who can guarantee a great one? Who can ensure you will make it through, with your ruby slippers on and your straw body intact? Who can be certain that the great wizard's voice you hear at times is not coming from an ordinary man behind a curtain?

When it comes down to it, the only thing you can rely on is each other—which honestly is one scary proposition. Sure, there are plenty of resources: marriage books, marriage seminars, marriage DVDs, and marriage counselors galore. But not one is willing to give a money-back guarantee. In fact, the only device that I have found to work consistently—and again, this comes from a man who fails more often than succeeds—the only instrument that has truly made a difference for Lia and me is the compass called Hope.

In those soul-searching moments, I'm surprised how few guarantees there really are. I put hope in my car and it breaks; I put hope in a job and I'm fired; I put hope in relationships and they change.

But there are a few things in which we can hope entirely.

The Newlywed Game, the newlywed life, the life we have fallen into, the place we find ourselves, is Hope. It is hope in each other. Hope in a future. Hope in being something greater than either one could be individually. It is hope that we are not alone, that others have gone before us, that Hope has entered within us, and that one day we'll see His promise.

Lia and I hope for more days like the ones we had on the cruise. Most days don't come close. And I wonder if that's okay. I wonder if something's wrong with us when days go by and I can't think of a single significant thing to write about in my journal.

Maybe Hope is the waiting time between those magical moments. On the days when I get nothing right, when everything she does is wrong, Hope is the glue that holds us together. Hope is the present experience of a future actuality. It's a certainty in those things unseen—like the certainty I have that those vows I can't keep will somehow be kept, and that all these newlywed questions will someday have answers.

Chapter Nineteen
Bad Hobbit

I was scarfing down vittles and heading for the door, but my stomach wasn't satisfied, and neither was my wife. Our five-minute dinner didn't seem to do either of us any good.

She was giving me one of those discontented looks, the kind she makes with slitty eyes and a crinkled nose, her glare chasing me around the house like the broad side of a broom.

It was Wednesday evening. I was late for practice, and she didn't like it—not that I was late, but that I had practice.

I played guitar in our church band. Church, I had found, was far more entertaining with an instrument in hand. But all good things cost something, and Sunday fun was costing me a Wednesday night and a hot-tempered wife.

Lia's least favorite times were the moments when our schedules didn't jive, when the one night she had nothing planned was the one night I did. It didn't matter where I was going; the mere fact that I was going at all ticked her off.

I had anticipated this and hoped to appease her by fixing her favorite foods for dinner: corn dogs, tater tots, and spinach salad with feta cheese and Craisins. (Lia is a culinary eclectic to the max—impossible to understand, easy to please, endearing all the way. You gotta love a woman who craves a corn dog, eats her potatoes nugget-sized, and likes her cheese crumbled.) But nothing was satiating her appetite tonight.

This was unfortunately becoming a theme—her getting held up at work and my committing to too many things. If it wasn't church band practice, it was band practice with The Shifty Fish (my garage band) or a soccer game across town or helping Frank paint his basement or … the examples were many. I basically said yes to anything fun, and she had had it up to here with all the promises to others I had to keep and all those to her I was breaking.

A particular sticking point that evening had been our inability once again to find an evening to see the final *Lord of the Rings*. She had brought it up for the umpteenth time while I washed down my tots with a last swig of milk. It had been in theaters for weeks already, and as we looked at our schedule for the week to come, there was no room for a three-hour movie.

It was definitely not happening tonight, I told her.

As I started collecting my equipment, I felt the sting of her words and her unsatisfied look as they chased me around the house. They stung while I grabbed my guitar case and when I opened the fridge to pick an apple for the road. I wedged it in my mouth like I was a pig to be roasted and muffled an insincere "I'm sorry" as I rushed by her to the door.

The air bit with cold as I walked to my car. My nose immediately started running, and there was a tingling sensation in my fingertips. I could feel the juice from the apple begin to freeze to my lips.

I wonder when it happened, when Adam realized he had made his fatal mistake. You know, with the apple. Did he feel a twinge of guilt before the shiny fruit touched his lips? Did he have any notion as his teeth broke the skin? Did he feel his throat tighten as the first morsel slid down? Did he get that gut-gurgling sensation

as the remnants lay in his belly? When did he know? Was it after it
was gone, after he had tossed the core in a bystanding shrub? Did he
think one bite would make such a difference, would change the rest
of history? Would he have done it if he had known it would cost so
much? Did he weigh the cost before he decided to take that bite?

No way. Adam was just like me, just like most guys I know. He
leapt before he looked, committed before he counted, swallowed
before he chewed, threw before he measured.

Apples did that to men; at least, they did for Adam and me.

So down the road I drove. I didn't feel much like church, didn't
have the heart, didn't like how I had left things with Lia. I hated not
meeting a need, especially when the need was me, especially when
the one in need was one whom I loved.

I merged onto I-25 South, turned on *All Things Considered*, and
listened to Robert Siegel. Driving with my knee, shifting with my
wrist, I munched away and cursed my tardiness.

I felt an impulse to call Lia as I passed under Hampden Avenue—to apologize sincerely, to tell her that I loved her and that my
actions would someday mirror my words. I had walked out and shut
the door, preoccupied and in mid-conversation. I had left the dishes
uncollected and unwashed, for her to deal with. If I were really
sorry, I wouldn't have left it like that. I would have let the band wait;
after all, who was more important?

I decided I would call and tell her I would do the dishes when I
returned. No, by now water would be running through her fingers
and her sponge. I was already too late to stop her. *I should call her
anyway*, I thought. My phone sat patiently on the passenger seat,
awaiting my command.

I reached over, but my apple, a golden delicious if I remember
correctly, was viced between my middle finger and thumb. I'd have
to finish it before I called. Who likes talking to a muncher? *You
know how Lia feels about chewing with your mouth open, and you can't*

rightly talk with your mouth closed, I reminded myself. I'd call once I got to the parking lot.

I turned on Holly Avenue. Mr. Siegel was introducing another story about Iraq. I was down to rabbit nibbles.

I pulled into a parking place; my phone looked up at me expectantly. "Okay, okay," I said, "just hold on a minute. Have to get myself situated." I opened the car door, placed the apple core on the roof, leaned my guitar against the side of the hood, and slid my phone in my jacket pocket. Shutting the door and grabbing the apple in my left hand, I searched for a place to toss it.

Twenty feet away lay a small grassy knoll, pocked with snow; a solitary pine crouched like a catcher a few feet from the curb.

Perfect.

And instantly, I turned into a kid. It's amazing how a target and an object to throw can change everything ... everything from the attitude of a heart to the very state of a marriage.

I was Steve "Lefty" Carlton, my childhood hero, and at the same time Harry Kalas, the legendary announcer for the Phillies, giving color commentary and context. In a poor, nasally impersonation, I described the scene: "Folks, hope you've been here to witness this. Steve Carlton has pitched a perfect nine-and-two-thirds innings. It all comes down to this: the bottom of the ninth, the count gone full. Reggie Jackson will not go down without a fight. Lefty's going to need the pitch of his life. Ozzie Virgil gives him the sign. Carlton shakes it off. Looks like he's going out on a limb; history hangs on the next two seconds. And here's the wind-up! THE PITCH ..."

I gave it all I had. The apple core soared ... a dead strike.

Ding.

What was that? A ding? Apples don't ding. Had I hit something? I looked around. Maybe somebody was walking on the sidewalk, practicing the triangle. Maybe my apple was metal on the inside.

Maybe ... no ... couldn't be ...

I looked down at my left hand. My ring was gone. My fingers had shrunk with the cold; my ring must have been loose—and man, I must have thrown hard! I shook my head in disbelief. Steve Carlton had pitched my wedding band away!

It was dark. The parking lot was faintly illuminated by austere, shaming lampposts, casting more shadows than light. I turned my car back on and clicked the high beams. Scanning the lot, I saw no silver glimmer. Not even a glim. I had never felt so dumb in my life.

I heaved one long sigh and felt my chest cavity press against my cell phone.

Oh boy, do I call Lia now?

Not on your life.

Instead, I went inside and told my band mates. We postponed practice and put on our jackets. Before heading outside, Michael, our leader, huddled us up and prayed for God to guide us. Drummer Dudley organized the search. Two in our search party switched on the headlights in their Suburbans; the sexton rustled up a couple of flashlights. With all this help, it would only take a second to find the ring—or so I thought.

Several fruitless minutes passed with no success (actually, we did locate the apple). It was cold, and folks were getting chilly, so they started shooting questions at me: Where, again, did you throw? And where did you hear this "ding"? Are you sure you were wearing your ring? Are you sure the ding wasn't in your head? I could hear two cold vocalists whispering "ding-dong" and giggling.

After ten minutes we had narrowed our search to somewhere east of the Front Range and west of Kansas. The wind had picked up; the same asphalt pebbles kept catching our eyes. I waved my naked hands and called off the search.

"It will be a lot easier to see in the daylight," I shouted.

At the utterance of such profound truth, we nodded philosophically and walked indoors.

Michael put his arm around me and, confessing for all to hear, shared how he had lost his wedding ring twice. His wife, our keyboardist, shook her head at the memory, but she was smiling. Our two lady vocalists added that they were both on their second diamonds. Drummer Dudley described how he had misplaced his for two and a half years before finding it in his golf bag. It seemed almost everybody had a story. In fact, losing your wedding ring appeared to be more a rite of passage than poor happenstance. My marriage wasn't doomed; I was now part of the club. No wonder you see all those old folks with metal detectors spending their retirement days scouring sandy beaches; they're looking for the wedding rings they lost!

As we packed to go, I started thinking again about Lia. How was I going to tell her? How was she going to react? I pictured her rummaging through the kitchen, deciding whether to attack me with a knife or bonk me on the head with a frying pan. *Maybe it will be better to wait. Anyway, she'll be in bed by the time I get home. No need to wake her.*

I wondered if I could hide my naked finger from her for twenty-four hours. I'd keep my hands in my pockets until she left for the hospital and then cruise down to church after work. If she called and asked what I was doing, I'd tell her I had to pick something up. It wouldn't even be a lie.

The whole thing seemed a lot funnier the second day. It really wasn't that big of a deal. Just a hunk of metal—I never liked it in the first place. That platinum rubbing against my middle and pinky fingers was something I had never gotten used to. Anyway, it wasn't like I was throwing away my marriage—just its symbol. And odds were I'd find it and have it back on my hand by dinner. Heck, maybe I'd even tell Lia what happened. She'd get a kick out of it.

We'd laugh at cocktail parties about the time I "flinged" my ring. We'd bend backward and laugh with our mouths in the air, our hands holding wine glasses, and our rings chinging the crystal. I'd quip how, for a while, there was no sign or token of my sign and to-ken of abiding love and undying devotion. My friends would really think I was witty.

The morning wind draped over Chelsea and me as we went on our morning walk, but I only sensed its chill in one tiny region—on the fourth finger of my left hand, between the knuckle and the palm. My ring finger was naked. It had grown sensitive during these years of protection. A sudden shudder coursed through my body as I realized that I missed my ring.

I missed looking down and seeing it. I missed feeling its weight. I missed spinning it like a coin on my lunch break. I missed trying to stop it mid-spin with my forefinger. I missed throwing it up in the air and trying to catch it like a hoop on my pinky. I missed clanking it against metal railings and hearing the chime.

When I had it I didn't like it, but now that it was gone I could hardly stop thinking about it. I missed my wedding ring. I wanted to get it back.

Work felt longer than usual, but once I was free, I sped to my car and down the highway, back to the scene of the fatal pitch.

I parked in the exact spot as the night before, planning to retrace my steps. Detaching a key ring from the others, I figured the best course of action was to reenact the previous night's event. So I dug my foot into a make-believe pitcher's mound, adjusted the invisible rim on my invisible baseball cap, wound up, and threw an imaginary apple core at yesterday's pine tree/Ozzie Virgil. The key ring sailed through the air and landed by the curb. Wow! It had flown farther than I expected. I decided to repeat the experiment: the metal circle landed almost exactly in the same area. I tried it a third time—same place. I looked up and down the general vicinity, fanning my fingers inch by inch over the cold winter grass. No revelation.

Hmmm. So what variables are unaccounted for in this experiment? I asked myself. Boy, I was going to need my old physics thinking cap. I hadn't worn that thing in a long time. Let's see … a platinum wedding ring was probably three times heavier than a stainless steel key ring, so multiply the distance by three. That would take my search over the parking lot, over the grassy knoll, and across the street! I whistled—that was a lot of space. I started walking in that direction when I remembered friction. I hadn't factored in friction. Now, my wedding ring had been a lot tighter on my finger than my key ring, so that would mean more friction and less distance. But how much less? And would the contact with my knuckle change the trajectory of the projectile? I sighed. Physics was expanding the possibilities, not narrowing them.

I eventually resolved to adopt the ancient farmer-tilling-his-field technique and spent the rest of daylight weaving back and forth, a few feet at a time, over a fifty-by-fifty-yard area. After an hour, the sun began dipping behind the Colorado Rockies, and with it, my chances. Opportunity vanished in the blanketing shadows.

I checked the time on my cell phone; Lia would soon be leaving the hospital. She'd be calling, and I'd have to tell her something. I pondered possible tactics: Maybe I could beat her home and sabotage our heater, requiring us to wear gloves and long underwear all night. No, she hates the cold so much, she'd make us stay in a hotel. Maybe I could wrap my hand in gauze and pretend I slammed it in my desk at work. Nah, she's a doc; she'd insist on looking at it. Hmmm. Maybe I could make up a story about a dog attacking Chelsea. The dog had gone for the jugular, and I fended the canine off with my left hand—but in the process my ring had slipped into its mouth. But I'd have to get some fake blood or something to make it look realistic, and she might insist I go to the emergency room and get a rabies shot ... argghh.

Could I tell her the truth?

It seemed too late for that. Truth had a small acceptance window, and after it closed it was better to lie. Small window ... yes! How could I have been so blind? Engagement! Proposals! I'll just buy another one! I'll just run and get a replacement at the mall.

I checked the time again. None to lose. I dashed to the car and turned the ignition.

At precisely the same moment, my phone vibrated to life.

It was Lia.

I paused, wondering whether or not to answer. It continued to ring. I sighed.

"Hello?" I answered.

"Hey, where are you?"

Where was I? Oh yeah. "I'm at the church. I had to pick something up."

"Did you find your ring?" she asked.

Did she just ask about my ring? "My what?" I asked.

"Your ring," she repeated.

"My ring? What's wrong with my ring?" I asked, trying to remain calm. How did she know? Had she inspected me last night while I was sleeping? I'll tell you—women. You can't fool them, not for an instant.

"Michael called me today and told me how you had lost it."

Michael! Now why would a man do such a thing? I was in for it. I gulped. "He did?"

"Yeah, he told me how upset you were and how you all had looked for so long. Is that what you were doing down at the church?"

"Maybe," I answered, still unsure how much truth was safe to divulge.

"Did you find it?"

The moment of truth. *Do I say yes and go to the mall, or no and come clean? Ugh, these are the things they should cover in marriage counseling.*

"No," I answered.

"That's okay." She didn't seem angry at all. "If we can't find it, we'll just get you another. Hurry up and get home. I canceled my meeting and picked up two tickets for *Lord of the Rings.*"

"Really?"

"Now come on. I'll fix a couple of corn dogs for the road."

Lia was fine. She understood. She had already forgiven me.

"I love you, Leela. I'm so sorry. I feel like an idiot. I would be the worst hobbit."

"Come home, Frodo," Lia said with true tenderness.

———————————

Every Sunday Lia and I take a symbolic stroll in a strip of grass, hoping one of us might catch a glint of metal. It's a favorite stroll of ours. We hold hands and feel each other's palms, her finger squeezing the substitute stainless steel that we bought for ten bucks after the movie.

Since the ring was so cheap, I had suggested buying two or three, just in case. Lia had shaken her head. "Let's take it one ring at a time."

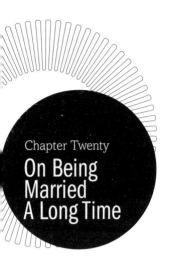

Chapter Twenty

On Being Married A Long Time

Let's see. Today is November 12, 2004. Lia and I have been married almost four and a half years—basically five. What is it that makes me want to round up? Do I think some prize is waiting behind each number scaled on the nuptial ladder?

By February of last year, Lia and I were already saying things like "we're going on four years" or "we've been married, oh, about four years" or "we'll be close to our fifth anniversary in about a year's time." Basically, as soon as we were able to, we rounded up.

Why is that? Why is being married a long time so cool? Being old isn't. A matronly woman will lie about her age and in the same breath brag about being married half a century. A man will complain about how long he has put up with his old lady, but with a sparkle in his eye affectionately announce his anniversary tally to all within earshot. It just doesn't add up.

Marriage isn't easy. Maybe that's it. Being married a long time is an achievement. Being married for thirty, forty, fifty years seems nearly miraculous.

It seems crazy—the marriage commitment, that is. What gave me the idea that I have what it takes to stay attached to the same person for the rest of my life? It took me years to stay in a relationship for more than three months—and even then I did it mostly out of principle—and both those relationships ended like Hiroshima. Was I out of my mind?

I can't commit to anything. I get hooked on a brand of cereal, and in no time I hate it. I begin a new hobby and lose interest in a week. I promise to prune the grapevine and leave it half done. I am not good at cleaning up scraps.

That's the story of my life—a pathway of destruction and unaddressed mess. Our marriage has never been pretty.

But five years is almost in rounding distance, and, strangely enough, we are still united. I still feel like a rookie, waiting for my first hit, still wondering if it will ever get hard and if it will ever get easy.

Lia, maybe we are fools. Maybe not. Guess only time will tell.

Chapter Twenty-One
Rash Love

It was Thanksgiving, going on Christmas, and I loved my wife for the first time. We were three days out from a four-day weekend and a cross-country flight to spend the holiday with my parents, and I discovered I could love. I know this might sound strange. Hadn't I loved Leela all along? Hadn't Love been baked into the brownies? Hadn't Love led our two-wheeled chariots across the bridge of acquaintance and into friendship? Hadn't Love compelled me to humiliate myself over the phone to Lia's parents? Hadn't Love allowed us to persevere through awful gift exchanges, ruined carpet, a coffee war, and a lost ring? Wasn't it Love who united Lia and me, Love who held our broken pieces together, Love who guided us by the compass called Hope?

But if marriage has taught me anything, it is that I stink at love. How loving is my wash-the-dishes, mow-the-lawn love? Am I not motivated by precaution and prevention? I serve, but do so out of fear, in order to evade wrath and sustain peace. What is my buy-her-flowers, say-sweet-things love? Again, I have an underlying intent: self-pleasure. It makes me feel good when Lia smiles, it makes my life better when Lia thinks I'm thoughtful, and it makes my odds for sex increase when Lia's smelling petals. But is that love? Do I love her, or do I love sex?

I'm not emotionless; I feel the feelings. I have a lot of passion when it comes to my bride, but what do you call actions instigated by a desire for self-preservation and self-satisfaction? Surely, you can't call it love.

The Bible says that love is patient, kind, not proud, and not self-seeking. What the heck do you call what I do? What do you call something that is impatient, prideful, self-seeking, and the opposite of kind?

King Hubris, King of Beasts: that's who I am.

Love is a foreign object to this animal. For me, love is an evolutionary third arm I do not have; love is a pair of wings on which natural selection flew by; love is somewhere in that part of the brain I do not use.

How do you manufacture a thing you cannot make? How do you find a thing you never lost? How do you open a gift you've never been given?

I'm asking—I don't have the answer—is love a gift or is love earned? If it's a gift, Lord, give it to me! If it's an acquisition, sign me up for the class!

Oh, I want love! I want real love. I may not have ever truly given or received it. But man, do I love the idea. And boy, do I want it: no-strings, no-agenda, no-conditions love. I want love more than I want to live.

And I want to love. I want to love someone other than myself. I want to love someone more than I love myself. It sounds so free-ing—to love without expecting in return, to give just because I can, to be rewarded simply by the pleasure of selflessness. I want to love that way. And to be honest, I want to be loved that way by others.

It sounds so simple. It seems so easy. Just love—find a woman and love her. But something—namely, somebody—gets in the way: me.

So what I do is something slightly less than love: I give, in order to get. And who I love, as a result, is none other than myself. And that is not love; that is self-absorption. That is self-love, and it merely leaves you unsatisfied and empty.

And so I try to love, and I stink at it. Never have I felt so unworthy, so incapable, and so poor at anything in my life. I am a failure at love—that is what marriage has taught me.

Therefore, it came as a surprise when I loved for the first time. What brought it on, you ask? Well, I will tell you: it was the rash. (To call it simply a "rash" does not do it justice, but the word I called it would have been inappropriate for publication.) It was a red, scaly, nasty-looking rash that was the catalyst to love.

The Monday before Thanksgiving we had some friends over for dinner. Lia had this garlic shrimp, veggie, and rice idea and was flying solo in the kitchen. I was given music and tidying duty, so I spent thirty seconds throwing clutter in a closet and thirty minutes crafting a soundtrack for the night.

Kerry and Kelly walked in with a handshake, a hug, and a bottle of wine. I took their coats and tossed them on our spare bed. Kerry uncorked the wine and poured us all glasses. Lia was waiting on simmering brown rice, so to coax us out of the kitchen, she spread a platter of cheese and crackers. But Kerry and Kelly, being lifer types, refused to leave the kitchen. Instead, they rolled up their sleeves, searching for ways to help. There was nothing to do, though, since Leela had done it all, so we leaned against the counter, holding wine in one hand and needless spatulas in the other, and began to share the humorous events of the day. Since Kerry, Kelly, and I didn't have much to relate—our lives are boring—Lia began telling us about the hospital, a place that provides all kinds of entertaining stories.

Over the weekend, Lia had been working on the wards. From the way she described the scene, the sick were hanging from the rafters. Flu season had arrived with force, knocking down the door and entering without permission or invitation. Lia said you could almost see the germs with their claws and tails scrambling around the place. You had to wear gowns and shower caps and face masks and gloves and get rid of them right after visiting with each patient. The hospital looked like Halloween, everyone walking around with sheets like ghosts, with only their eyes exposed. But even with all that protection, you still felt contaminated, she said. You'd check a child's throat for inflammation, and inches from your face he would cough. You could feel the tiny spit globules landing in your cornea and the microscopic germ monsters digging into your body, riding your veins like a roller coaster.

Her stories were always the best. After the coughs, the snots, the lurching, it was a miracle we were still hungry.

We topped off our glasses.

Lia asked me to sample the rice. Lifting the handle, I looked down at the little buggers. As my forehead began to sweat from the steam, my imagination took hold, and suddenly the rice took on personality and life. I pictured macroscopic germs like evil pills of poison, a pile of monsters steaming and hissing and waiting to dig into my body and ride my veins like roller coasters.

I swallowed hard. I put the lid back on and told Lia the rice looked ready. She asked me to bring it over and I obeyed, trying to shake the images from my cranium. Keeping my mouth shut, I spooned rice onto Kerry, Kelly, and Lia's plates, then gulped and spooned a mound onto my own.

We sat down and toasted grace. Our eyes circled the table and spoke gratitude.

Lia's meal was fantastic—the shrimp pink and succulent, the veggies steamed to perfection. We offered a barrage of compliments to a chef becoming increasingly red in the face. Lia was laughing, the way she does when she is embarrassed. We marveled at her modesty: "Lia, you really are a very good cook. The dinner is delicious."

Conversation continued, shifting from Lia's cooking to government conspiracy theories, a favorite topic of Kerry's. I shared about a television show Lia and I had once watched about the moon landing. We had been convinced for a whole twenty-four hours that we, the United States, had not landed on the moon, but rather had taken all those pictures in a Hollywood studio. Conversation then shifted to hotter topics, like the war in Iraq. Kerry asked what we thought would happen if we never found weapons of mass destruction. Lia got very red and started shaking. Noticing her complexion, Kerry assumed he had touched a nerve and suggested we change the subject. I agreed.

"Lia, are you okay?" asked Kelly.

Lia sat silent. Her blush was turning blotchy, accentuating itself in places, like above her right eyebrow. She resembled a crimson version of Violet Beauregarde from *Charlie and the Chocolate Factory*. It was sudden and awful. Leela was metamorphosing before our very eyes. Our dear lifer-type friends were speechless, as was I.

Lia's eyes filled with water; I could tell she was embarrassed. Clearly, she was not looking well.

"Maybe it'd be best if we hung out another time. I think I need to lie down," she said, helping us out of our dumbness.

We all agreed.

I collected coats. Kerry and Kelly said they'd call us before we left town. I watched them leave from the front door, waited until their brake lights glowed the color of Lia's face, and reentered the living room. Lia was lying down, the back of her hand covering her eyes. She looked dead.

Now, this is when I started to surprise myself. Usually I would say something stupid like "You look nasty" or "I hope it's not contagious." But I didn't. Instead, I walked to the couch and gently placed my hand on her hair. She was breathing quietly, so I returned to the dining nook, carried the dishes to the sink, washed them, and cleaned the counters—all on my own initiative.

I went back to my wife and asked if she needed anything. She asked for Benadryl, so I got her some. I filled a small cup of water and arrived at her side with the medication. Placing a pill in her rashy palm, I rested her shoulder blades on my knee. She asked if I would take her to bed, which at times means one thing, but this night meant another. I was happy, just the same.

I led her to our bedroom. She asked if I would read to her, so I willingly obliged and read words until her breathing had that sleep sound in it. From my pillow position beside her, I watched her body slowly rise and fall. Beyond her the clock read eight o'clock. I was missing *Monday Night Football*. For some reason, however, I preferred to watch Leela this evening. Stretching, careful not to disturb her, I extinguished the light over her head. I listened in the darkness, curled beside her, and shut my eyes for the next ten hours.

The next morning she looked bad, and by bad I mean gross and disgusting. She showed me her stomach. It reminded me of Mars—bumps, craters, and red all over. I hugged her.

Lia called in sick the next two days but went to the hospital, where colleagues tested her for everything from mononucleosis to lupus. And while they waited for the test results, her doctor addressed Lia's epidermal abnormality by prescribing Atarax, an allergy drug literally on steroids. I picked it up at the pharmacy on the way home from work.

The medicine acted fast, sending her into a stupor and sapping the rest of her energy. We sat across from each other and she updated me on her condition. We wouldn't know the test results until tomorrow. She asked how my day was. I said, "It was fi—."

She was asleep before I finished the sentence. I paused, but then decided to continue talking to Lia anyway. I whispered all the events of my day with as much detail as I could remember, with only minor embellishments here and there to add a little flavor. The crooks of her mouth curved toward her ears as she breathed.

After a couple hours, I managed to wake her enough to feed her some food, help her with her pajamas, and slide her into bed before she was out again for good. I spent another night by her side.

She was sleeping when I left the next day. I kissed her corrosive temple and told her I'd be back as soon as possible. She mumbled a moan.

The doctor called mid-morning. She didn't have mono or lupus or anything they could identify, which was comforting and discomforting all at once. So during Lia's few minutes of lucidity, she did her best to diagnose herself, believing by the end of an hour that she had something called *erythema multiforme* (Google that and click on some photos if you want to see something sick).

I left work at lunch. When I arrived home, she drunkenly described her disease to me. It sounded pretty awful. Groggily, she apologized that she wasn't being any fun, and I responded that watching her migrating hives was entertainment enough. She lifted her shirt, exposing the new locations where the inflammation had sprouted. I said I thought she was being a great sport about this; she said I was the great sport.

"Do you think we should cancel our flight to Philadelphia?" I asked her.

"Ned, we've been looking forward to seeing your parents for months."

"But I don't think we should go if you're not feeling up to it."

"That's very sweet," she said, "but I'm feeling a lot better today, even if I don't look it. Anyway, the plane won't be bad—with the drugs I'm taking, I'll be sleeping the entire way."

"Are you sure?" I asked.

"Sure, I'm sure."

I was glad. I really did want to go home for Thanksgiving.

By some miracle, Lia's rash had all but vanished Thanksgiving morning, so she decided to hold off on the Atarax. If she took it she might not be able to stay awake long enough to make it through security.

"Are you sure that's a good idea?" I asked. She nodded.

We drove early, parked our car in the Mount Elbert lot of Denver International Airport, shuttled to the Frontier kiosk, checked in, passed through screening, and arrived at our gate with time to spare. Traveling on Thanksgiving was going to be easy. With the time difference, we'd cross the country just in time to sit down to turkey.

Once aboard, we found our seats. Lia took a blanket, a pillow, and the window, and I found myself next to a cool Buddhist telekinetic/spiritual medium who kept me company.

(I have heard it said that 25 percent of airline travelers hope to find a soul mate, or at least a date, while on board. Another 25 percent are looking for a new friend. The final 50 percent desire to do nothing but sleep, read, or just be alone. Ashamedly, pre-Lia, I was one of the hopeless romantic types. Post-Lia, I land solidly in the find-a-friend pie wedge. However, on long flights, I usually keep to myself, at least for a while.)

On this day, I waited until Pittsburgh to begin talking with my new Buddhist buddy. He was very interesting. And I was firing questions as fast as I could think them: How do you tell the difference between good energy and bad energy? What do ghosts look like? What do dead people like to talk about? What's the spookiest movie you've ever watched?

Lia had been trying to sleep since St. Louis. Every time she was almost asleep, her bottom jaw would drop and her lips would make a tiny pop, and the sensation would cause her to wake. Not to mention that her rash was coming back with a vengeance.

Lia tapped my arm and looked at me for help.

"Do you want to take an Atarax?" I asked.

"I can't take it on an empty stomach," she replied.

"Oh."

I didn't know what to do, so I turned to Buddhist Buddy, who was looking past me to Lia with an eyebrow raised in concern. From his countenance, I could guess he had never seen a ghost, spirit, or force as spooky as my wife.

I told him that I didn't think it was contagious. At least, I hadn't contracted it yet.

His wide eyes told me he didn't believe me.

My eyes told his he might be right.

The arrival into Philadelphia was pretty turbulent. Buddhist Buddy and I had contracted some bad energy during the final descent; we were both turning green. Lia was green and red mixed together, which doesn't make much of a color at all. Needless to say, we were all thanking our Higher Powers at touchdown.

As we feared what might physically come out of our mouths if we opened them, we didn't have many words to say to each other as we parted ways. I hope Buddhist Buddy had a good Thanksgiving. Lia and I would have a memorable one.

Surprisingly, our bag was the first one on the belt. "'There's a first time for everything,' my dad always says." I wondered if our baggage good fortune was a sign of things to come. "Let's see if he is waiting for us."

"I sure hope so," said Lia.

We called Pops to swing around, pick us up, and take us to turkey. He was just circling around to baggage claim. We were heading home in record time.

Next to our front door resides a holly tree that's probably ten years older than me. When my family moved in I was three, and she was already a tree. Every few years she grew enough red berries to downweigh her arms. I used to pluck them and practice my jump shot while waiting for my ride to school. Pops spent many an afternoon pruning her off our front porch. If I listen to my memory, I can vividly hear the shrill scrape of holly prickles scratching designs into the metal of our front door. She wasn't a very attractive tree, sort of boxy—not the kind you'd see on a postcard.

Growing up, I had felt a lot like her—branches too big for the plot of land in which I was planted. I was a rebel with prickles who never took too kindly to pruning. It got pretty hairy for a couple of years, but eventually good won over evil. For a long time, I could not think of anything better than to leave this place. Years later, I could hardly think of a better place to be. Coming home makes me contemplate; it makes me listen and reflect and interpret. Mom and Pops loved me enough to let me go, and, by grace or luck, their prodigal found his way.

From the looks of it, they had adopted the same principle with Holly Tree. She was looking finer than ever, with her branches spreading free. And as I opened the door, I felt her familiar points press through my fleece. I guess Mom and Pops had grown accustomed to using the garage entrance.

My hands full of bags, I held the door with my knees for Pops, who walked in carrying the rest of our luggage, and then Lia, who entered carrying a disease.

Rae, my seventeen-year-old nearly blind, nearly deaf, nearly bald dog, sniffed my ankles and wagged her tail. She was the first in the line of greeters who had assembled in our foyer. Next was my sister, a smile covering her face; her husband, stretching his ready hand in greeting and saying hello in one of the twelve languages he knows; their two kids, Rebecca and Joshua; my sister's in-laws from Maryland, their daughter, and her fiancé; Jeff and Stacy, two of our best friends who were too far from their own families for the holiday; their baby boy, bouncing like a beach ball against Stacy's stomach; my Aunt Dawnie, who is single and available and has dimples; and finally, my mother, her eyes shining sweeter than their chocolate color. Thirteen people in all. I could feel Lia's exhaustion as she faced the line of grinners; I could see her energy fading by the time she squatted down to acknowledge her niece.

"Momma, what's wrong with her face?" asked Rebecca.

"Rebecca, that's just the way she looks today," said my sis.

"But Momma, her face is scary."

Joshua must have agreed; he was peeking an eye at his monstrous aunt from behind his mother's knees.

"Sorry," said Sis to Lia.

"It's okay. I know I don't look so well."

Everyone drew in like fair-goers at a freak show.

Lia was about to crumble.

"Hey, Mom, how about some dinner?" I shouted to break up the awestruck crowd.

"Coming right up," she answered. "Make your way to the table."

And disaster was averted—for the time being.

My mom and her apron make one heck of a Thanksgiving dinner. Besides a turkey cooked to perfection, Mom makes her stuffing with homemade bread. It is so good she makes double portions; it's the kind of delicacy that people fight over. In all my years of eating, her stuffing has gone unrivaled. But that's just the tip of the iceberg.

Then come her mashed potatoes, whipped with a dollop of sour cream, an ice-cream scoop of butter pooling in the middle like the setting of a sun. Beside that is a bowl of gravy, steaming like a morning lake. Next to these are the Erickson traditions—mashed yams with browned marshmallow topping, brussels sprouts bobbing in liquid butter, cranberry sauce that only my father likes, and rutabaga, which everybody likes. The Thanksgiving spread is the incarnation of happiness, which is the emotion I feel just about every Thanksgiving Day. It makes me happy to know that a place is set for me. It makes me happy to be in a ring of friends and family. Happiness swirls through my arms and into my chest as we hold hands and thank God for the food we are about to eat.

But I wasn't happy yet.

"Do you think you can make it?" I asked Lia in her ear once I had dropped our bags inside the door.

"Yes," she answered, sounding unconvinced.

"Do you want to take your drugs?"

"I think I'll be okay."

I wondered if I should tell her how bad she looked.

"Not yet," she amended, referring to the drugs.

She took wobbly steps toward the dining room and changed her mind again: "Ned, maybe you should get me a pill."

One by one we each found the place set just for us. Sitting in a ring of friends and family, we held each other's hands, thanking God for the food we were about to eat. And in an instant, food and compliments were being passed around and everyone was doing their best not to stare at Lia's rash.

But it was unavoidable. She was puffy, with red patches as if her skin were stained with cherry Kool-Aid, and splotchy, like a dashboard under a streetlight in the rain. It looked like her body had been overcome by molten-lava ooze.

We were all looking. We tried not to notice, but we couldn't help it—Leela was turning colors before our very eyes. Poor Leela—she hated being center stage; she avoided it like the plague. But there was nothing to be done. The plague was on her face.

"I think I need to lie down," she announced, and instantly we sprung into action as if we had just been waiting for the word, which, of course, was what we had been doing.

Dishes were getting stacked, scraps Tupperwared, counters scrubbed. Pops rushed to the family room, mounded cushions, and snapped the sleeper-sofa in place. Mom and Dawnie harvested pillows and blankets.

Lia held my arm as we walked through the kitchen. Her eyes, like a heavy cloud, thundered, and the tears fell all at once. After three days of feeling bad, her body finally broke down.

"Why?" she sobbed. "What is going on with me? Why is this happening?"

I didn't know what to say.

Lia looked at me, helpless—which is exactly how I felt.

"Do something, Ned."

"Lia, I—"

"I know you can't. I've ruined everything, haven't I?"

"You're not ruining anything."

"I've ruined your ... I'm going to throw up."

And up and out it went: turkey, stuffing, mashed potatoes, gravy, yams, brussels sprouts, cranberries, rutabaga, and all. I caught some in the hand; the rest I caught in my shirt. We veered into the bathroom where the toilet took my place. I heeled the door behind us, knelt beside my bride, and held her hair as she heaved her guts out.

"I'm sorry," she kept repeating, in between convulsions.

"For what?" I finally asked, when the storm had subsided.

"For being so ugly."

"Come on, now. I don't think you're ugly."

"Yes, I am. Look at me."

"So what?"

"What if I stay like this for the rest of my life?"

"I wouldn't care."

"Yes, you would. I'm hideous."

"Lia, I really don't think I would," I said, as honest as truth.

For a second she believed.

"Do you still love me?" she asked.

"Now more than ever."

I dabbed the sweat that had collected in her temple; she smiled through shut eyes.

"Will you read to me?"

"You bet."

I went into the family room and found her pajamas and a new set of clothes for me. After informing the family that Lia was making her way to bed and was going to be fine, I changed our clothes and carried her to the sleeper-sofa. By the time I began to read, her breathing had gotten the sleeping sound in it. I read on anyway. And as I read to her, I realized I could love—love the way I wanted to: no strings, no agenda, no conditions. It was nothing I had done; I had merely fallen into it.

Over the years, I've discovered a lot of things. I've discovered I can prune grapevines and never clean up the mess. I've discovered I chew with my mouth open. I've discovered I hate to make the bed. I've discovered words or actions are not enough on their own. I've discovered people can tell when I'm uninterested in what they are saying. I've discovered I think I'm a lot cooler than others do. I've discovered I am evil and can think evil things. I've discovered attraction to other women doesn't go away. But I've discovered I would rather stick with the one I've got. And I've discovered I'm not alone in these discoveries.

I've discovered sex is harder than it looks in the movies. I've discovered I can cook more than eggs and honey toast. I've discovered I can cough and remain asleep, but I cannot sleep through the sound of someone else grinding her teeth. I've discovered I can dust and clean, but it is better to get a maid. I've discovered I laugh when I orgasm. I've discovered there's more pleasure in giving Lia one.

I've discovered my wife can make me feel better and worse than anyone else on the planet, and that I can do the same to her. I've discovered I simultaneously feel afraid and excited at the prospect of having kids. I've discovered I have never known another person as intimately as I know this woman, and yet I'll never know her fully. I've discovered I can't imagine a future without Leela. And just recently, I've discovered I can love. Even if it is momentary. But I've discovered that when love flees, fidelity remains and hope remains and the fruits of love remain, and love will come again.

Lia's rash remained for ten days. I'll spare you the details. She now thinks it was simply *urticaria* (a fancy word for hives) that gave her spots like a giraffe, the result of some viral reaction from some monster germ that rode her veins like a roller coaster. But she still isn't sure. And perhaps it will be something she will always be susceptible to. In fact, a few days ago, her skin flared up again. Maybe she will stay like this for the rest of her life.

It was Christmas Eve. Lia was at the Children's Hospital of Denver working another thirty-hour shift. I was thinking about gifts because I was staring at them under our four-foot fake tree. There were three boxes with my name. One looked like a card deck; I picked it up and found it to be surprisingly heavy. Ah! My magnetic poetry! I lifted a bigger box, and it rattled like a jigsaw puzzle—glow-in-the-dark ceiling stars! She had remembered. The third present was the largest, big enough to hold three plain T-shirts of different colors.

I put all three gifts back down on the coffee table, which Ryan, my last roommate before Lia, had left me. Our feet crossed upon it, we had been talking about the Braves when he told me I could keep it. Now I crossed my feet upon it again and leaned back into a couch. This couch had been a gift too. My grandparents had given us the money to buy it when we got married. My eyes scanned the room; practically everything I could see had been given to us.

Was everything a gift?

My heart said yes.

Marriage was a gift. Life was a gift. Love was a gift. Everything we had was a long and wide and high and deep parade of gratuity. Given, not earned.

I stewed on this for a while, and eventually came back to the rash. The best gift this Christmas was the feeling I got when I kissed her swollen cheek, the happiness I felt as I read to her at night, the joy I would receive when she opened the camera I had bought her with money I had secretly earned—the one she said she wanted but said we couldn't afford.

The greatest gift is giving, isn't it? Not getting love, but giving it; not getting life, but sacrificing it; not getting a wife, but being a husband. Love and Life and Marriage are best when they are given with no strings, no agenda, and no conditions.

And so, Leela, I love you. I love you for putting up with me these going-on five years. I'm optimistic about the next five, hopeful about the next ten, and dreamy about the next half-century. Not because I've done anything to deserve a life with you, but because the things I long for are gifts. And so they are things I cannot earn, only receive. Come what may. Come rash, come all.

Chapter Twenty-Two

Just Breathing ...
Just Like Breathing

I just dreamed about my grandpa. He hasn't been alive for several years now.

He was my hero. I suppose most grandfathers are. They have perfect laps, they tell the best stories, and they have magic pockets always full of spare change. Grandpa had these—these and much more. Not for a second have I doubted that he was the greatest man who ever lived, though I'm not sure how I came to this conclusion. However, as I dreamed, I believe I saw the reason. I witnessed the poetry that was his life.

Let me paint the scene. Before me rose a three-story Victorian home with creamy blue siding, white shutters with wooden slats, a porch that wrapped all the way around like a belt, steps that led out to a lush and long field of grass—a perfect croquet lawn—trees lining the sides, a bell tower like one you'd see at a college in England. I had never been here before, yet I knew it was my home.

I walked into the parlor. Grandpa was standing in the curve of a bay window, a folded paper in hand, singing in a tone too low for me to make out the words—he always had a rumble in his baritone. My mother, his oldest daughter, walked into the room and into his arms. He sang a soft song into her ear—the words on the folded paper, I knew. They rocked back and forth, eyes closed. Mom had never looked so beautiful. In a flash, they were dancing, spinning and swirling and laughing. With one hand Grandpa held hers; with the other he held her waist. My mother's feet were floating.

As the quiet serenade drew out slowly, Grandpa dipped Mom so low that her hair touched the floor and her right foot rose like a counterbalance. She was smiling to her ears when Grandpa drew her back upright. He tightened his hold for a drawn-out moment, relaxed, then stepped away. He said, "Madam, with your permission I must retire. I am required in the library."

He bowed and handed her the folded paper. Mom began reading, and tears filled her eyes; one released and landed on the paper. It made a print like a butter stain.

Grandpa left her in the parlor and walked into the library.

I followed. As I entered, Grandpa was slumped in a rocking chair. In his older years he had developed a hunch in his back from too many days typing journal articles for engineering magazines or bending to kiss his grandchildren or carrying burdens like we all do. A folded paper rested in his hand while he rocked to a tempo in his heart. Was he sleeping?

Dawnie, his second daughter, entered the room. She was younger than I had ever known her—a teenager, I think. By the time my eyes returned to Grandpa, he was out of the chair and waiting for her. She collapsed into his arms, upset about something that had just happened. He held her and whispered, in a tone only she could hear, the words on the folded paper. They rocked back and forth, eyes closed, Dawnie's face lost in the fabric of his flannel.

When their sway had lost momentum, Grandpa held her. Her crying turned to breathing, and their breathing joined cadence, steady and gentle like waves on a windless day. He tightened his hold for a drawn-out moment, relaxed, then stepped away. "Madam, with your permission I must retire. I am required in the sunroom."

He bowed and handed her the folded paper. She curled into the rocking chair and spread the letter in her two hands; she admired it with eyes bright as Christmas morning.

Grandpa left her in the parlor and walked into the sunroom.

By the time I entered, Grandpa was sweating, sick, suffering on a couch. There was a nurse dabbing his forehead with a wet towel. Grandpa was on his side, his right arm on his chest like a boomerang, his left dangling off the side of the couch, a folded paper crinkled in his fingers.

Melanie, his youngest daughter, entered the sunroom. She was five years old. Her yellow hair flared above the shoulders; her yellow dress flared above the knees. Her father looked more like her grandfather—they must have been at least seventy years apart! Immediately, as she walked through the doorframe, Grandpa sat up and looked well again. I searched, but the nurse had vanished. Only father and daughter were in the room.

He smiled and patted the cushion beside him. Mel skipped to his side and sat deeply into the couch so that her knees could not bend and her patent-leather shoes stuck straight out. He began to speak, arms accenting the words. He was reciting the words on the folded paper, describing in the most grandiose terms his deep affection for her. She giggled and grinned; her cheeks beamed. When he was finished, she turned her chin up to his face, completely enamored.

Grandpa placed his hand on her yellow head and left it there for a moment, then leaned down and kissed her before standing up. He turned to his daughter and said, "Madam, with your permission I must retire. I am required in the great room."

He bowed and handed her the folded paper, which she took and placed to her heart. Grandpa left her in the sunroom and walked toward the great room.

Grandma must have met him on the way; they were arm in arm as I watched them enter. They were the age I remember them best—Grandma, her gray hair wrapped in a bun, wearing one of her husband's shirts; Grandpa, silver streaks combed back and to the side, wearing his flannel shirt and cowboy jeans. They walked around the great room, looking at pictures, at books, at gifts, at objects that awakened memories—the symbols of a tremendous life. They made their way to their favorite spot, the windows facing the west.

All of a sudden, I realized we were back in Missouri, back on their ranch. I watched the colors of their clothes melt to gray as they looked toward the Ozark hills, the sun painting their silhouettes against the sky. They looked like two doves folded in each other's wings. They remained there long past sunset. The sky changed from pink and orange to purple and then black. Stars rubbed their eyes and began to blink. I could barely see them, but out of the stillness, I heard Grandpa stir. He unbuttoned his chest pocket and, with two fingers, like tweezers, clasped a folded paper within.

He said, "Madam, with your permission I must retire. I am required in the study." He continued to hold her.

Finally, he bowed and handed her the folded paper. It hurt to see them part; it didn't seem right for him to leave her. Grandpa left her in the great room, and I began to cry.

When I walked into the study, Grandpa was sitting away from the entrance. His head bobbed up and down to heavy breathing. He was asleep. I tiptoed to his side. We were alone in the room. In his lap lay an open Bible. I couldn't make out chapter and verse; the light was too soft. But when I looked upon his face, all I could see was Love.

"Teach me to love," I whispered. I don't think he heard me. Maybe he did. He did not reply.

Instead, he breathed, just breathed, his Bible like a blanket. He breathed like he had entered a land of dreams, a world of horses and riding and cattle to round, a world of magic and miracles and mystery, a world more real than any I have known.

And the dream must have been good, for there was light upon his face. He had fallen into Love, and it was just like breathing. Just like breathing. Just like breathing.

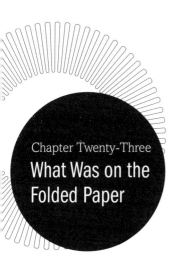

Chapter Twenty-Three
What Was on the Folded Paper

I awoke. It was three in the morning, but I knew I would sleep no more that night. Lia was facing away from me, lying on her side. There was no sound to her breathing.

I thought about Grandpa and Grandma, and I thought about the dream I had just had. There was something there I needed to pay attention to—something in Grandpa's words, something in his steps, something in the way he related to the women in his life, in the way he danced with my mother and rocked with my aunt and talked to their sister. There was something in the way he held his wife. There was something in his countenance as he lay there in his study.

As quietly as I could, I tiptoed to the door and wove my way through our dark house. I entered our study and typed the events of the dream as best I could remember them, the words that appear in the previous chapter.

I read them over and over, and then I realized what it was. I realized that Grandpa, eyes closed, arms folded, his Bible like a blanket, had answered me.

He just breathed.

"Love like you breathe," he said. "Love like it is the most natural thing. Love like your life depends on it."

Inhale. Exhale. Love is breathing in and breathing out. It is being loved and loving, being forgiven and forgiving, being served and serving. Love is receiving and giving. It is receiving grace and giving grace. It is being sacrificed for, and it is laying down our lives for others. In and out. Just like breathing.

It was quiet in our house. I heard the gentle hum of the refrigerator and the push of air from the vents on the floor. The almost imperceptible buzz of electrical current coursed through the lamp above my head and the computer at my fingertips. A rectangle of light skated across the walls from a lonesome car driving down Colorado Avenue. The light paused as the vehicle pulled up to the stop sign just outside the window, then dashed away. The sound of the engine faded into the gentle hums and the imperceptible buzzes, but I was not alone. Grandpa was there with me, he and a cloud of witnesses.

I leaned back into my chair, wondering what was written on those folded pieces of paper. A word? A poem? A love letter? Perfect words in perfect prose? A story for the ages?

I wished I had it in me to write something like that.

"Teach me the words, Grandpa," I whispered.

"Breathe, Ned," I could hear Grandpa say.

"Breathe, I got it—but what were the words?"

"Just breathe," he said.

I still did not understand.

"Just breathe."

"I don't know how," I said.

"Breathe like it is the most natural thing. Breathe because your life depends on it. Breathe because it is all you can do."

"Grandpa, I do not understand."

I could feel him coming close, could almost sense his hand upon my shoulder.

"Breathe about a brownie bet and a cockroach named Fred. Breathe about tears by the sea and a phone call and a broken rock and a breakfast in the sky. Breathe about a ruined carpet and a skeleton suit and a coffee war and a newlywed game and a lost ring and a rash."

"But that's not love. That's just what happened."

"Precisely. Love happens."

"So what was in the folded paper was a story?"

"It was my story, the one that happened to me."

It couldn't be. Grandpa was eighty-two when he died. He had traveled the world, loved to the full, lived a dozen lives. There was too much to write, too many stories to tell, and not enough space to tell them.

"But how did you fit your story on a single piece of paper?" I asked.

He smiled. There was a twinkle in his eye.

"Magic."

Notes

1. Jimmy Soul, "If You Wanna Be Happy," *If You Wanna Be Happy: The Very Best of Jimmy Soul* (UK: Ace Records, 1996).

2. Fyodor Dostoevsky, *The Brothers Karamazov* (New York: Signet Classics, 1957), 106.

3. BrainyQuote, "Confucius Quotes," BrainyMedia, *http://www.brainyquote.com/ quotes/authors/c/confucius.html* (accessed January 19, 2005).

4. The History Channel, "The History of Valentine's Day," *http://www.historychannel .com/exhibits/valentine/* (accessed January 19, 2005); "Valentine's Day History," *http://wwwpictureframes.co.uk/pages/saint_valentine.htm* (accessed January 19, 2005).

5. Del Amitri, "Never Enough," *Twisted* (A&M Records, 1995).

6. The Churchill Centre, "Speeches & Quotes," *http://www.winstonchurchill.org/i4a/ pages/index.cfm?pageid=388* (accessed January 17, 2005).

7. Miku B. Sippy, "Said with Koffee," BMI Global Consultants Ltd, *http://www .koffeekorner.com/quotes.htm* (accessed January 31, 2004).

Discussion Guide

Reading can be magical. The magic happens when the words cause us to remember something from our own lives. The magic happens when the words cause us to reflect and go further beneath the surface. The magic happens when the words cause us to respond, when they encourage us to live or think differently. Use the following questions to help you remember, reflect, and respond.

Chapter 1: Sure Bet
Remember:
• Retell the story of how you and your significant other first met.
Reflect:
• What were the circumstances that were outside of your control that brought you two together?
Respond:
• How do you interpret things that are outside of your control?
• What does this say about what you believe?

Chapter 2: Cousin Fred
Remember:
• When was the first time you noticed your significant other's beauty?
Reflect:
• When, if ever, do you think it is appropriate or right to keep things from each other? How has secret-keeping played out in your relationship?
Respond:
• Do you think there is such a thing as "the one"?
• What are the implications of that belief?

Chapter 3: Treasure
Remember:
• Have you ever had a *Goonies* moment (when you shared all your baggage) with your significant other? What happened?
Reflect:
• Is it possible not to carry our past like a hump on our back?
• How has your history affected your relationship for better or worse?
Respond:
• Do you think you are a treasure?
• What makes this hard to believe? What convinces you it is true?
• How could the way you perceive your value affect how you live?

Chapters 4 and 5: The Dumbest Thing I Have Ever Done and The Most Humiliating Moment of My Life

Remember:
- What happened when you asked for the father's blessing?
- Share the most humiliating moment in your relationship.

Reflect:
- How is your relationship with your in-laws? Why is it easy or difficult to relate to them?

Respond:
"Our stories, our lives aren't necessary ... And yet my story happened ... and so did yours. You are here; you are alive. And that's significant" (28).
- What is the difference between being necessary and being significant?
- Do you believe your life is not necessary?
- What makes your life significant?

Chapter 6: Engagement

Remember:
- What was the engagement period of your relationship like?
- What marital advice did you receive? What did you do with it?

Reflect:
- Which engagement metaphor, of the ones Ned used, do you relate to most?

Respond:
"Engagement is our life—or a lot like our life" (49).
- How is engagement like life?

Chapter 7: The Beauty Battle

Remember:
- What was pre-marriage counseling like for you?
- How was it helpful or unhelpful?

Reflect:
- When you look in the mirror, what do you see?
- How does self-image affect your relationship?

Respond:
- What are ways you can help yourself and your significant other "break open"?

Chapter 8: Gifts

Remember:
- What was the worst gift your significant other ever gave you?
- What was the best?

Reflect:
- Which is harder for you: receiving or getting gifts? Why?

Respond:
- Share what gifts, in general, mean to you.
- Talk about ways you can make giving and receiving gifts more special.

Chapter 9: Valentine's Day Massacre

Remember:
• Who was your Stephanie Fitzpatrick (your first crush)?
• What has been your experience with this most evil of holidays?

Reflect:
"Why can't one perfect day of romance be enough? …We all want more. We always want more. We are never loved enough" (87).
• Is this true? Is there such a thing as being loved enough?
• How does your need for love affect your relationship?

Respond:
• What do you think of Ned's theory on our infinite need for love? (88) What do you believe?

Chapter 10: New Carpet

Remember:
• Do you agree with Ned and Lia's categorical system of friendship?
• Was there a time when you spent too long with a friend and nearly sabotaged the relationship?

Reflect:
• Who was your hero growing up? What did you love about him or her?

Respond:
• Where have you seen "beauty in the brokenness"?

Chapters 11 and 12: How Lia Got Her Nickname and Why Ned Hates His Pet Name

Remember:
• Do you have a nickname or pet name? How did it come about?

Reflect:
• Why are the names we call each other significant?

Respond:
"'Sometimes,' she said, 'courage for me is getting out of bed'" (99).
• What is courage to you?

Chapter 13: Typical Conversations: Going Out to Dinner

Remember:
• What does a typical conversation about choosing a dinner locale sound like in your family?

Reflect:
"You're just supposed to know. If you take the time to make sure we are on the same page, you will just know" (106).
• What value do you place on your significant other's ability to know you?

Respond:
• What are ways you can communicate better with your significant other?

Chapter 14: The Best Smell
Remember:
• How does hygiene, or lack thereof, play out in your relationship?
Reflect:
• Does Ned have a point in saying there is an intrinsic problem in the fact that we spend so much of our time and money on changing the way we smell?
• How does smell affect the way we perceive reality?
Respond:
• Is it important to support the manhood/womanhood of our significant other?
• What are proper ways we can encourage each other to be manly or feminine?

Chapter 15: The Bachelor
Remember:
• What television program do you secretly love or fight over?
Reflect:
• Why are we so intrigued by love stories? What does that say about human nature?
Respond:
• Does one's heart have a mind of its own? Can you control whom it falls to? If so, how? If not, does your heart always lead in the right direction?

Chapter 16: The Coffee War
Remember:
• What attributes or habits have you tried to change in your significant other?
• How have you fared?
Reflect:
• Are there healthy ways to address the bad habits of your spouse?
• What are they? Or is it a helpless cause?
Respond:
"When God handed us the puzzle pieces of our hearts, He withheld one—a piece in the shape of Himself" (121).
• Do you think we have missing parts that need to be filled?
• What are your missing parts? Which ones have been filled?

Chapter 17: Chomping to the Oldies
Remember:
• What was your best road trip?
Reflect:
• How do you deal with the habits of your significant other that drive you crazy? What should you do?
Respond:
• Spend some time dreaming up a road adventure for the two of you.

Chapter 18: Newlywed Game
Remember:
• Answer the newlywed questions that Ned and Leela had to answer (if you are

in a group, try playing the game!) (150-151).
Reflect:
• Share some of your "greatest marriage moments."
Respond:
• What is your definition of hope? What are things you put your hope in?
• What are things you can hope in entirely?
• How is hope like a compass in your relationship?

Chapter 19: Bad Hobbit
Remember:
• If you have ever lost your wedding ring, share the story.
• If it hasn't happened yet, who will lose it first?
Reflect:
• How does busyness affect your relationship with each other?
Respond:
• Why is forgiveness so powerful? Why is confession so hard?
• If necessary, take some time to confess and forgive each other.

Chapter 20: On Being Married a Long Time
Remember:
• Do you round up when telling people how long you've been married? Why?
Reflect:
• Is commitment difficult for you? Why or why not?
Respond:
• What do you want your marriage to look like in ten years? Thirty? Fifty?

Chapter 21: Rash Love
Remember:
• Have there been times in your marriage when you have loved with no strings, no agendas, and no conditions?
Reflect:
• Is love something that just happens to you? Or is love something that you make happen?
• Is love a state of being or an action? Or a little bit of both?
Respond:
"Over the years, I've discovered a lot of things" (180).
• What would be on your list of discoveries?

Chapters 22 and 23: Just Breathing … Just Like Breathing and What Was on the Folded Paper
Remember:
• Have you ever had a life-changing dream?
Reflect:
• How is love like breathing?
Respond:
• What would be on your folded paper?

[RELEVANT BOOKS]

For more information about
other RELEVANT Books,
check out www.relevantbooks.com.